YOU KANT MAKE IT UP!

"A tasty smorgasbord of problems, which belie their apparent simplicity by getting to the heart of what it is to reflect on the world philosophically."

Martin Cohen, author of *101 Philosophy Problems*

"Lively and entertaining. It shows some great philosophers at their weirdest and wonderful best."

Peter Cave, author of *Can A Robot Be Human?*

"A delightful read. Fun and informative."

William Irwin, Professor of Philosophy, King's College Pennsylvania

ABOUT THE AUTHOR

Gary Hayden is a journalist and popular philosopher. He has a master's degree in philosophy and has written for *The Times Educational Supplement* and numerous magazines. He is the author of *This Book Does Not Exist: Adventures in the Paradoxical*.

You Kant Make It Up

Strange Ideas from History's Great Philosophers

Gary Hayden

ONEWORLD

A Oneworld Book

First published by Oneworld Publications 2011
Reprinted 2011, 2014, 2018, 2019

ISBN 978–1–85168–845–6 (Paperback)
ISBN 978–1–85168–907–1 (Special Hardback)

Typeset by Jayvee, Trivandrum, India
Cover design by BoldandNoble.com
Printed and bound in Great Britain by Clays Ltd, Elcograf S.p.A.

Oneworld Publications
10 Bloomsbury Street
London
WC1B 3SR
England

Stay up to date with the latest books,
special offers, and exclusive content from
Oneworld with our newsletter

Sign up on our website
www.oneworld-publications.com

This book is dedicated to my Dad

CONTENTS

'One cannot conceive anything so strange and so implausible that it has not already been said by one philosopher or another.'

René Descartes

INTRODUCTION

Philosophers are clever folk. Some of them outrageously so. Yet they say the strangest things!

Take the German philosopher Gottfried Leibniz. He designed calculating machines; invented calculus independently of Isaac Newton; and made important contributions in physics, logic, history, librarianship and theology. He could hardly have *been* any cleverer. Yet he claimed that objects don't really have shapes and sizes; and that the world couldn't possibly be any better than it is.

Or consider the French philosopher, Blaise Pascal. He did groundbreaking work in vacuum physics; invented the syringe; gave the world 'Pascal's Triangle'; and was one of the founders of probability theory. Yet he said that you ought to believe in God even if you doubt His existence.

Why so strange?

Philosophy abounds with strange ideas. As you read this book, you'll discover that history's deepest thinkers have claimed that matter doesn't exist; that unicorns *do* exist; that babies deserve Hell; and that your mind doesn't influence your behaviour.

But why? What is it about philosophy that gives rise to so much weirdness? And how is it that such brilliant people can say such outrageous things? Is it because genius and craziness are so closely linked? Or is there some other reason?

Well, perhaps the main reason for all the weirdness lies in the nature of philosophy itself. Philosophy concerns itself with ultimate questions. This means that philosophers sometimes find themselves operating at the very limits of thought; at the very edge of what is thinkable. And this can be a very strange place.

Think of those cutting-edge physicists who try to figure out what goes on at the quantum level or at the centre of a black hole. They paint a picture of a world very much at odds with the world of common sense. A world where space and time get warped; where fundamental particles pop into and out of existence; and where multiple universes spring into being.

Philosophers are a bit like that. They too ask deep and difficult questions. The kinds of questions that stretch the understanding to its limits – and beyond. *How are minds related to bodies? Can we ever be absolutely certain of anything? What, if anything, is the point of life? What makes some actions 'right' and others 'wrong'? If there's a God, what kind of being must God be?*

In investigating these questions, philosophers take themselves outside the ordinary trammel of thought. So it is hardly surprising that they come up with some very strange-sounding ideas.

Ways of being weird

The ideas in this book are all strange. But they're strange in a variety of ways. Some of them, like John Locke's claim that oranges aren't orange, seem plainly wrong. Others, like St Thomas Aquinas's insistence that masturbation is worse than rape, are deeply shocking. Still others, like Pythagoras' claim that 'everything is number', don't even seem to make sense.

Some of the ideas seem strange when you first encounter them but not so strange once you stop and think about them. A number were considered outrageous when they were first proposed, but have since become quite mainstream (amongst philosophers, at any rate). All of which brings us to an important point . . .

Strange but true?

Strange ideas aren't necessarily *wrong* ideas.

As you read this book you'll come across ideas that will surprise you, amuse you, offend you and confuse you. But you'll also come across ideas that will convince you. Sometimes you'll find yourself nodding in agreement, and accepting ideas you never thought you *could* accept.

So be warned. A couple of hundred pages from now you may have acquired a firm belief that oranges aren't orange; that matter doesn't exist; that Harry Potter *does* exist; and that this isn't the real world.

Using this book

I've arranged this book into forty-three self-contained chapters, each one dealing with a single idea. The topics covered include ethics, logic, politics, metaphysics, psychology, sex and religion. On balance, it's probably best to read the chapters in order, and allow yourself time for reflection between each one. But that's not essential. There's nothing to stop you from hopping around, or reading the whole book in one splurge, if you prefer.

I've begun each chapter by introducing a strange idea and then giving some of the arguments that a famous philosopher has advanced in its favour. Wherever possible, I've done that in a way that's fairly sympathetic to the philosopher's views. After that, I've generally offered some criticisms; some arguments that cast doubt on the philosopher's idea. Overall, I've tried to stay impartial so that you can decide for yourself what you make of it all.

At the end of each chapter I've provided pointers to related chapters. These are for the benefit of those of you who like to hop around where your interests lead you. At the end of the book I've offered some suggestions for further reading. So if you find a particular philosopher or a particular idea especially interesting, you'll be able to find out more.

1

NOT *BAD*. JUST MISGUIDED

The Greek philosopher Socrates (*c.*469–399 BC) placed great faith in the power of human reason. He believed that reason, properly cultivated, will make us virtuous and happy; that once we truly know what is good we will do it; and that anyone who acts wrongly does so only through ignorance.

The sceptics among us might well wonder what planet Socrates was living on. We know from bitter experience just how impotent reason can be, and what an immense gulf there is between knowing what's right and actually doing it.

The voice of reason

Of course, we wouldn't expect a philosopher of Socrates' stature to make such an outrageous-sounding claim without having his reasons. And, indeed, he did have his reasons. His supporting argument runs as follows.

We are all *hedonists*. That is, everything we do is prompted by the desire to experience pleasure or to avoid pain. This means that all talk of 'good' and 'bad' ultimately boils down to considerations of pleasure and pain. Whatever leads to pleasure we call 'good'; and whatever leads to pain we call 'bad'.

Clearly, no one knowingly chooses pain over pleasure. But this is equivalent to saying that no one knowingly chooses the bad over the good (since the terms are interchangeable). Therefore, anyone who *does* choose the bad in preference to the good must do so in error: because he mistakes it for the good.

Sound reasoners, then, will always do what is good for *themselves*. But will their wisdom also make them virtuous? Will it lead them to treat *others* well too? Socrates thought so. Here's why. Acting unjustly, he said, is harmful not only to those we wrong but also to ourselves. When we act unjustly we damage our own souls. So doing what is right toward others is doing the right thing for ourselves too.

The voice of experience

Socrates claimed, then, that when we truly know what is good we will do it; that knowledge is virtue. The obvious rejoinder is that his argument cannot be sound since its conclusion is palpably false. People *do* very often choose the bad – even when they know it to be bad.

For example, a morbidly obese person may be in no doubt that his high-fat, high-sugar diet is ruining his health, making him unattractive and damaging his self-esteem. But his knowledge is impotent. Time after time, he finds himself knowingly choosing the bad in preference to the good.

Socrates' response

Socrates anticipated this objection. He said: '[Most people] suppose that though present in a man, often not knowledge but something else is in control – now high spirits, now pleasure, now pain, sometimes sexual desire, and often fear.'

But, he insisted, the problem in such cases is not that knowledge is impotent, but rather that what appears to be knowledge isn't really knowledge at all. Anyone who chooses a wrong course of action does so only because he is not truly convinced that it *is* the wrong course of action.

How could Socrates know this? Well, because we are all hedonists and will therefore always choose the greatest quantity of pleasure and the least quantity of pain – *provided we do our calculations correctly*. It is simply absurd to suppose that anyone will knowingly choose the lesser pleasure or the greater pain. Therefore wrong choices simply *must* be the result of miscalculation.

If the morbidly obese man truly understood the nature of his choice, and was skilful enough in calculating its consequences, he would choose the seafood salad in preference to the burger and chips every time.

No true Scotsman

Socrates here seems guilty of using the No-True-Scotsman Move: an intellectual dodge designed to protect one's claims from being falsified by counter-example. The No-True-Scotsman Move was identified and labelled by the British philosopher Antony Flew (1923–2010) in his 1977 book, *Thinking Straight*. A simple example goes like this:

John: No Scotsman puts sugar on his porridge.

Jane: But Angus McSporran's a Scotsman, and *he* puts sugar on his porridge.

John: Maybe so. But no *true* Scotsman puts sugar on his porridge!

Isn't this pretty much what Socrates does?

Socrates: Anyone who knows the good will choose it.

Phaedo: But Jonathan McGreedy knows the good, and he doesn't choose it.

Socrates: Ah, but if he *truly* knew the good he would certainly choose it.

21. OUCH! I FEEL GOOD ➡

30. NO ONE'S TO BLAME ➡

43. THE UNEXAMINED LIFE ➡

2

COULDN'T BE BETTER

Any reasonable person must concede that in many respects the world is a bit rubbish. Joy and beauty there may be; but there is also ugliness, anguish and pain. This poses a problem for *theists* (those who believe in an all-powerful, all-knowing, wholly benevolent God) since if God is all He's cracked up to be, why has He created such a second-rate world?

The German philosopher and mathematician Gottfried Leibniz (1646–1716), a theist through and through, was acutely aware of this problem and addressed it in his 1710 work, the *Theodicy*. He presented the anti-theist's challenge along the following lines:

1. If God were all-powerful, all-knowing and wholly benevolent then He would create the best of all possible worlds.

2. But this is no way the best of all possible worlds.

3. Therefore God isn't all-powerful, all-knowing and wholly benevolent.

Possible worlds

What is meant by all this talk of 'possible worlds'? Well, there are an infinite number of ways the world might conceivably have been. Each of these worlds is possible, and therefore God might have created it, provided that it is logically consistent. (Not even an all-powerful God can create a logically *in*consistent world: for example, one in which two plus two equals five; or one identical to ours in every respect, including pig-physiology and the laws of physics, in which pigs fly.)

One way to think about this is to visualise some of the ways our world might have been. For example, this book might have had an extra chapter; the 2010 Haiti earthquake might never have happened; pigs might fly; and so on. These worlds of the imagination are all (provided they pass the test of logical consistency) possible worlds. In addition, there are any number of possible worlds so different from ours that the imagination balks at them.

Best possible world

Having cleared that up, we can now examine Leibniz's response to the anti-theistic argument stated above. God's reputation survives unscathed, Leibniz said, because this world, the one we inhabit, is the most perfect there can be. This *is* the best of all possible worlds!

This seems outrageous. Can Leibniz seriously have claimed that no world could possibly be any better than this one? How about a world with less pain, disease and suffering? How about, to take a specific example, a world in which a 2010 earthquake doesn't lead to hundreds of thousands of deaths and untold misery in Haiti?

In the *Theodicy*, Leibniz responded to this objection in two ways. First, he pointed out that although we can conceive, easily enough, of individual aspects of the world that might be improved, we are incapable of judging what the knock-on effects might be. Changes that appear to be for the better may, in fact, make things worse overall. God, on the other hand, sees everything, and, taking everything into account, creates the world with the highest possible ratio of good to bad.

Take mankind's capacity to do evil, for example. There's no doubt that this is the cause of much misery and suffering. God could, it seems, have created a world without moral evil but only by depriving us of free will. And since free will is, in Leibniz's view, a superlative good, such a world would be inferior to the world we inhabit.

Second, Leibniz said that the standards we use to judge the merits of possible worlds are too parochial. We tend to judge purely in terms of human happiness whereas God applies other, richer, criteria. One of Leibniz's suggestions is that from God's perspective the best possible world would be the one in which the maximum variety of phenomena are produced by the simplest set of natural laws.

Fair enough. Let's allow that for argument's sake. But even so, how could Leibniz be sure that *this* world, with its precise ratio of phenomena and laws, and its precise admixture of good and evil, is the best there can possibly be?

This *must* be the best

This is his reply: 'I do not believe that a world without evil, preferable in order to ours, is possible; otherwise it would have been preferred. It is necessary to believe that the mixture of evil has produced the greatest possible good: otherwise the evil would not have been permitted.'

In other words:

1. If God were all-powerful, all-knowing and wholly benevolent then he would create the best of all possible worlds.

2. But God *is* all-powerful, all-knowing and wholly benevolent.

3. Therefore this *is* the best of all possible worlds.

Leibniz turned the anti-theistic argument on its head: a piece of metaphysical manoeuvring so audacious that it brings to mind the story of the girl who murdered her parents and then asked the judge to have pity on a poor orphan.

3. COULDN'T BE WORSE

20. LEIBNIZ'S FANTASTIC FAIRYTALE

3

COULDN'T BE WORSE

The German philosopher Arthur Schopenhauer (1788–1860) is one of the gloomiest, most curmudgeonly thinkers of all time. His philosophy is uncompromisingly bleak and depressing. Yet, for all that, he is tremendous fun to read. Unlike his fellow countrymen, Kant and Hegel, he wrote beautifully; and he had a wonderful – albeit wickedly sarcastic – sense of humour.

Pain and boredom

Schopenhauer saw human life as a pendulum swinging back and forth between pain and boredom. We spend our lives craving things (wealth, status, artistic achievement, love, etc.) and suffer the agonies of unfilled desire until we attain them. But when we finally do attain them they lose their lustre. We quickly become bored with the very things we once craved.

'[The will's] desires are unlimited,' he wrote, 'its claims

inexhaustible, and every satisfied desire gives birth to a new one. No possible satisfaction in the world could suffice to still its craving, set a final goal to its demands, and fill the bottomless pit of its heart.'

The world as will

Schopenhauer claimed that the entire phenomenal world (the world as it appears to the senses) is a manifestation of will. What does this mean? Well, here's the gist of the idea.

We can know and understand our own actions in two different ways:

1. like any other phenomena, in terms of cause and effect;

2. more immediately, as acts of will explicable by motives.

Now, just as my bodily actions are manifestations of *my will*, in the same way all other phenomena are manifestations of *will in general*.

Will is thus the grounding of all things. Ultimately, everything is an expression of the universal will. But unlike my will, which is driven by motives, will in general has no motive. It is blind and purposeless.

Worst of all worlds

In the previous chapter we saw how Leibniz's belief in an all-powerful, all-knowing and wholly benevolent creator led him to the view that this is the best of all possible worlds. Schopenhauer, unsurprisingly, rejected this idea. 'The absurdity is glaring,' he wrote.

Schopenhauer's view of reality as the product of blind will led him to a very different conclusion. The world is horrible. It would have been better had it – and we – never existed.

In fact, not content with saying that the world is bad, Schopenhauer made the bolder, and considerably more entertaining, claim that the world is just as bad as it can possibly be. His supporting argument appears in volume 2 of *The World as Will and Idea*:

> Now this world is arranged as it had to be if it were to be capable of continuing with great difficulty to exist; if it were a little worse, it would be no longer capable of continuing to exist. Consequently, since a worse world could not continue to exist, it is absolutely impossible; and so this world itself is the worst of all possible worlds.

The argument is clever and amusing. But it rests upon a very dubious premise, namely that the world we inhabit totters on the very edge of annihilation; that the slightest change for the worse would render it completely unsustainable.

Schopenhauer cited various items of evidence in support of this claim. For example, he said that 'nine-tenths of mankind live in constant conflict with want, always balancing themselves with difficulty and effort on the brink of destruction'. And he claimed that a tiny alteration in the planet's orbit would extinguish all life on earth.

Examples of this kind may convince us that life on earth is fragile, and may even persuade us that the world is a pretty crappy place. But they fall far short of convincing us that the tiniest change for the worse would make the world's continued existence untenable. Hence, they fail to convince us that this is the worst of all possible worlds.

Schopenhauer assures us that he presents his proof 'seriously and honestly'. However, I can't help but picture him saying this with a mischievous twinkle in his eyes. That's just my opinion, of course. Perhaps he was deadly serious.

 **2. COULDN'T BE BETTER**

23. AN END TO SUFFERING

4

SELFISH MOTIVES

Does anyone ever perform a truly unselfish act? Surely the answer is yes. Every day we see examples of altruism and benevolence. People donate money to charity, volunteer time to worthwhile causes and perform acts of kindness towards strangers. And yet there is a school of thought known as *psychological egoism* which holds that none of these acts is truly altruistic; that they're all ultimately grounded in self-interest. But what selfish motives could anyone possibly have for performing them? This question was addressed by the English philosopher Thomas Hobbes (1588–1679).

Human nature

Hobbes is best known for his political work *Leviathan*, in which he set forth a 'science of politics' – a blueprint for establishing a peaceful society. He began by identifying some basic facts about human nature, which he then used to predict how people would react to various circumstances. This, in turn, allowed him to prescribe a scientific form of government which will reliably lead to peace and security.

The view of human nature from which Hobbes began is not a flattering one. He viewed individuals as greedy, competitive and aggressive. He wrote, '[I]f any two men desire the same thing, which nevertheless they cannot both enjoy, they become enemies; and . . . endeavour to destroy or subdue one another.'

The origin of altruism

Given that Hobbes viewed individuals as greedy and selfish, one might wonder how he accounted for the kinds of benevolent acts previously mentioned. His answer is that they are, in fact, motivated by self-interest.

How so? Well, Hobbes said that in addition to being greedy and aggressive, people are also reasonable. They are capable of thinking about where their best interests lie. For example, they can see that unbridled greed and aggression lead to conflict and war, which endangers their lives. Therefore they are willing to show regard for others in order to secure peace and safety for themselves.

Building upon the unlikely foundation of individual self-interest, Hobbes proceeded to rebuild the entire moral code. In the dedication to his work, *On the Citizen*, he wrote: 'From these starting points [human greed and human reason] I believe

I have demonstrated by the most evident inference . . . the necessity of agreements and of keeping faith, and thence the Elements of moral virtue and civil duties.'

Helping others – selfishly

Hobbes himself had a reputation for generosity and charitable giving. The antiquarian and writer John Aubrey gave a charming first-hand account of an occasion when Hobbes dug deep into his own pockets to relieve the distress of a beggar. This has every appearance of being an altruistic act, but Hobbes insisted that it was selfishly motivated: 'I was in paine to consider the miserable condition of the old man; and now my almes, giving him some reliefe, doth also ease me.'

All apparently selfless acts can be similarly reinterpreted. The young man who volunteers at the soup kitchen does so to feel good about himself and impress his friends. The mother who spends sleepless nights tending to a sick child is driven to do so by her own emotional needs. The soldier who saves his comrades by throwing himself on a grenade is prompted by a deep desire to think of himself, and be thought of by others, as a hero.

Every act is a selfish act

So psychological egoists like Hobbes hold a more subtle theory than at first appears. They do not make the palpably false claim that people never act benevolently, but rather maintain that benevolent actions, properly understood, are grounded in self-interest.

It is, in fact, possible to construct an argument that all actions *must* ultimately be self-interested. It runs as follows. Any act you perform voluntarily must be such that, on balance, you want to do it. Ultimately, then, you act to satisfy your own desires, which means that ultimately you act out of self-interest.

Fancy footwork

But there seems to be some fancy footwork going on here. When confronted with actions that appear benevolent the psychological egoist simply shifts the focus from outward behaviours to inner motivations. But inner motivations are private things, not open to inspection. The psychological egoist, then, appears to be doing nothing more than making an *assumption* about human motivation – one that cannot be tested, confirmed or falsified. When presented with *any behaviour at all*, she will insist that it is self-interested. Why? Because that is the assumption on which she operates.

John: What that guy just did was clearly unselfish.

Jane: No, it *appeared* to be unselfish. But, actually, he had selfish motives.

John: How can you possibly know that?

Jane: Because all actions *are* selfishly motivated.

The argument that everything you do voluntarily must be something that you want to do, and is therefore selfishly motivated, is equally dubious. It assumes that you can't have non-self-interested desires; that everything you want, you want for selfish reasons. But this is the very issue under discussion. It cannot simply be assumed.

25. SELFISHNESS IS A VIRTUE ⮕

5

NOTHING CHANGES

The universe is a single, unvarying ball of being. There's no past and no future. Nothing moves and nothing changes.

These are not the ravings of some obscure crank or crackpot. They are the carefully considered, closely argued claims of the ancient Greek philosopher Parmenides, one of the most influential thinkers ever.

Pioneer of reason

Parmenides (*fl.* fifth century BC) was born in the Greek colony of Elea on the southern coast of Italy. Very little is known about his life. And, indeed, not a great deal is known about his work. All that survives are some fragments, totalling 150 lines, of a poem that originally ran to perhaps 3,000 lines.

Parmenides earned his place in the philosophical hall of fame by being the first thinker to use strict reasoning to justify his metaphysical claims. Like many of his contemporaries he expressed his ideas in poetic form. But unlike them, he wasn't content with putting forward ideas that were merely interesting or plausible. He built up his theories logically, step by step, using meticulous argument. He *justified* his claims.

Parmenides' poem, *On Nature*, has been described as the first known attempt at systematic proof in Western philosophy. A huge achievement, by any standard.

Nothing changes

It's not easy to translate or to interpret Parmenides' writings. This is partly because he expressed his thoughts through poetry, and partly because, being a pioneer in the method of systematic proof, he sometimes struggled to find appropriate words to express his ideas.

Even so, certain features of his thought are clear enough. His fundamental precept was that *what is, is; and what is not, is not*. From this he deduced that things can neither come into nor go out of being. Why not? Well, they can't come *into* being because this would mean coming from that which is not. And that which is not, is not; it doesn't exist. Similarly, things can't go *out of* being because that would mean becoming nothing. And nothing, by its very nature, doesn't exist.

He further deduced that the world is one thing, and not many. Why so? Because if the world were many things then each thing would have to be separated from the others by non-being; by emptiness. And non-being cannot exist because that which is not, is not.

Similar considerations reveal that nothing moves. Here's why. For a thing to move it must go into empty space. But empty space is where that which *is*, is not. In other words, it is where only that which *is not* exists. But that which is not, is not. So there can be no empty space.

Change is also ruled out. This is because whenever you think, or express a thought, you think *of* something. In other words, your thought refers to something outside yourself. But you can think of or refer to that precise same thing at *any* time. Therefore it must exist in precisely the same way at all times. So nothing changes.

The supremacy of reason

There are many ways in which we might take issue with Parmenides. We might, for example, accuse him of playing with or misusing words – or at least of placing too much emphasis on them. Words and phrases such as 'is', 'is not', 'exists' and 'does not exist' appear simple. But they are, in fact, very tricky to handle. To see that this is so, you have only to consider a statement like 'the tooth fairy doesn't exist'. It seems perfectly straightforward but it's a philosophical minefield. This is because in order to say that the tooth fairy doesn't exist you have to refer to her. But since you can refer to her, it is tempting to think that she must, in some sense, exist after all.

But the most natural objection to Parmenides' view of reality is that it blatantly contradicts the evidence of our senses. He insisted that the world is one thing, motionless and changeless. But we only have to look around us to see that the world contains many things which are sometimes in motion and are subject to change.

Parmenides freely admitted this, but contended that reason is superior to the senses. If reason and the senses contradict one another then so much the worse for the senses. We must, Parmenides insisted, follow the arguments wherever they lead.

Reason demonstrates the world to be one thing and changeless; the senses suggest that the world is many things and changing. But reason is supreme. Only the intellect reveals things as they really are. The world of sight, hearing, touch, taste and smell is mere illusion.

Parmenides' ideas have been enormously influential. Most of the philosophers that came immediately after him devoted their energies to trying to reconcile his thesis that nothing changes with the seemingly contradictory evidence of the senses. Leucippus and Democritus, for example, explained the changing phenomena of the world in terms of the activity of unchanging atoms.

More importantly, Parmenides' method of strict argument and his recognition of the distinction between appearance and reality have remained central to the philosophical enterprise right down to the present day.

6. NOTHING STAYS THE SAME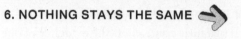

29. HARRY POTTER EXISTS

6

NOTHING STAYS THE SAME

Little is known for certain about the Greek philosopher Heraclitus (535–475 BC). But it is generally agreed that he was an arrogant and unpopular man. In *Lives and Opinions of Eminent Philosophers*, the third-century biographer Diogenes Laertius tells us that Heraclitus' misanthropy eventually led him to shun society and live off grasses and plants in the mountains. His ideas survive only in fragments attributed to him by later writers.

Heraclitus famously declared, 'Into the same rivers we do and do not step.' This is a very enigmatic statement and there's some debate over precisely what he meant. But his point seems to have been something along the following lines.

A river is made of water. Flowing water. This means that the physical make up of a river changes from one moment to the next. The water that makes up a river at one instant isn't the same as the water that makes up the river at another. So although we can step twice into a river, we can't, strictly speaking, step twice into the *same* river. Rivers have the intriguing feature that they're defined by change. Change is part and parcel of their identity. A river that remains static isn't a river at all. It's something else. Perhaps a pond or a lake.

Everything changes

This, in itself, is a fascinating insight. But Heraclitus had something more profound to share. He maintained that *everything* changes just as rivers do. 'The sun is . . . not only new each day but forms continually new', he said; and, 'It [is not] possible to touch a mortal substance twice.'

Modern science supports this notion. The desk I'm sitting at is made of wood. If I touch it twice, am I touching the same desk? In a sense, yes; but in another sense, no. How so? Well, scientists assure us that although wooden desks appear solid and static they are, in fact, composed of billions of sub-atomic particles all in ceaseless motion, and perhaps even popping into and out of existence. So although I can touch my desk twice, I cannot, strictly speaking, touch the *same* desk twice. Everything changes. Or, as Heraclitus put it, 'Nothing is; everything is becoming.'

Everyone changes

What is true of rivers and desks is equally true of human beings. Our lives, too, are characterised by change. Heraclitus appreciated this, and followed up his observation that we cannot step twice into the same river with the words, 'We are and we are not.'

Change is part and parcel of our nature. Throughout the course of our lives we change physically and we change mentally. When we compare what we are now with what we once were, it seems that we both are and are not the same.

What Heraclitus, through his enigmatic and obscure statements, seems to be suggesting is that things are not defined by their material constitution but rather by an underlying principle of change. It is in changing that things remain the same. This is a strange and even paradoxical concept, but it can be illustrated by means of a nice practical example.

The Ship of Theseus

According to legend, Theseus was an Athenian youth who sailed to Crete and fought a half-man half-bull creature known as the Minotaur. After vanquishing the monster, Theseus returned to Athens where his ship was preserved as a lasting memorial to his heroism.

As time passed, parts of the wooden ship began to decay and had to be replaced. Eventually, so many pieces had been replaced that it was unclear how much of the original ship remained. This led the Athenian philosophers to question whether or not the much-repaired ship ought still to be regarded as the Ship of Theseus.

This is a tricky puzzle, especially since we can imagine a time when every single plank of the original ship has been replaced by new timber. In what sense, then, can it be said to be the same ship? Most people, after some reflection, are willing to accept that the ship can retain its identity despite radical changes in its material constitution provided those changes are made smoothly and gradually, one or two pieces at a time. The key concept is continuity.

The changes that occur in rivers, in the sun, in everyday objects and even in our physical bodies are very much like the changes undergone by the Ship of Theseus. Everything is in constant flux. But the changes are underpinned by law-like principles that ensure continuity and order. So, even as things change, they remain the same.

A modern twist

There's a modern twist to the Ship of Theseus puzzle which makes it even more interesting, and which illustrates nicely the paradoxical element in Heraclitus' thought. In this version, as each decaying plank is replaced, it is taken away and used to create another vessel. So now there are two ships that can lay claim to the title, Ship of Theseus:

1. the seaworthy one constructed by gradually replacing parts from the original vessel;

2. the decaying one reconstructed from the original material.

The seaworthy ship lays claim to the title for the reasons already described, which are to do with continuity. The rotting ship lays claim to the title because it is made from the original materials and to the original specifications. This modern puzzle generates a lot of debate amongst philosophers about the roles that *spatiotemporal continuity* and *material constitution* play in enabling objects to persist through time.

The Ship of Theseus puzzle was probably devised after Heraclitus' time. He was, however, sensitive to the issues raised in even the modern version. 'Into the same rivers we *do* and *do not* step', he said; and 'We *are* and we *are not*.' So he recognised that both spatiotemporal continuity and material constitution enter into our ordinary ways of thinking and speaking about the persistence of objects.

Ordinary ways of speaking apart, though, Heraclitus regarded continuity as the true principle that enables objects to persist. Because no object ever *does*, in fact, retain all of its component parts, completely unchanged, from one moment to the next.

 5. NOTHING CHANGES

 23. AN END TO SUFFERING

7

TOTAL PERFECTION

In 1063 a Benedictine monk named Anselm was made prior at the Abbey of Bec in Normandy (he later rose, very reluctantly, to the dizzy heights of Archbishop of Canterbury.) The office involved him in numerous burdensome duties but he still found time to indulge his passion for philosophical and theological study.

At this time, Anselm conceived an idea that quickly grew into an obsession. He wished to discover a single argument that would prove beyond all doubt the existence of God. The idea took such a hold on him that he became neglectful of his other duties and began to wonder if the whole enterprise was a temptation from the Devil.

Eventually, however, he succeeded in formulating an argument that satisfied him. The fruit of his labours, now known as the ontological argument (Greek: *ontos* = being; *logos*

= knowledge), has been debated by philosophers and theologians ever since. It purports to show that God exists, by definition.

Anselm's greatest imaginable being

Anselm's ontological argument goes like this. God can be defined as 'a being than which nothing greater can be conceived'. In other words, as the greatest imaginable being. Even the 'Fool' (Psalm 14:1) who says there is no God understands this concept. Therefore the Fool must admit that the greatest imaginable being exists at least in his mind. Now, that which exists in reality is obviously greater than that which exists only in the mind. Therefore, if the greatest imaginable being exists only in the mind, it is possible to conceive of a greater being, namely one that exists in reality also. But this is absurd. One thereby conceives of a being greater than the greatest imaginable being. To avoid this absurdity we must accept that God exists not only in the mind but also in reality.

Having established God's existence, Anselm used the ontological argument to demonstrate other aspects of the Divine nature. He reasoned that it is better to be omnipotent, omniscient, merciful, etc. than not to be those things. Therefore the greatest imaginable being, God, must be all of them.

This is rather a convoluted argument. Most people, when they meet it for the first time, find themselves reading and re-reading it just to make sense of it. Basically, Anselm was saying that to exist in reality is better than to exist only in the mind. Therefore the greatest imaginable being must exist in reality.

Descartes' supremely perfect being

In the fifth of his *Meditations*, the French philosopher René Descartes (1596–1650) put forward his own version of the ontological argument. In addition to being a first-rate philosopher Descartes was a renowned mathematician. One consequence of this is that he generally presented his arguments with great clarity and precision. The ontological argument is a case in point. His version is much easier to follow than Anselm's.

He defined God as 'a supremely perfect being', and claimed that since existence is a perfection God must, by definition, exist. '[I]t is not less absurd to think of God (that is, a supremely perfect being) lacking existence (that is, lacking a certain perfection), than to think of a hill without a valley.' Just as it follows from the definition of a triangle that the sum of its interior angles must equal two right angles, so it follows from the definition of God that God necessarily exists.

Gaunilo's island

The first critic of the ontological argument was one of Anselm's contemporaries, a monk named Gaunilo. He said that Anselm's argument was clearly faulty since one could use essentially the same reasoning to demonstrate the existence of a perfect *anything* – for example, the most perfect island imaginable.

Anselm responded that the argument applies to God alone. Here's why. The concept of a being than which nothing greater can be conceived is a very clear and unambiguous one. Using it, we can, as it were, 'discover' God. We can reason our way to a knowledge of His existence and attributes. But we have no such clear and unambiguous concept of a perfect island, and therefore cannot apply the same reasoning to it.

Kant's objection

The German philosopher Immanuel Kant (1724–1804) also rejected the ontological argument. He said that existence is not a predicate. In other words, it is not a property that a thing can either possess or lack. When we say that something exists we do not add anything to the concept of that thing; we merely claim that there is something in the world corresponding to that concept. Since existence is not the kind of thing that God (or anything else) can possess or lack, the ontological argument never gets off the ground.

Was Kant right to claim that existence is not a predicate? Well, this is a rather technical question. Suffice it to say that most, but not all, philosophers agree with him that it isn't.

The hypnotic power of the ontological argument

The ontological argument has fascinated philosophers for almost a thousand years. So despite its oddity it must have something going for it. I first came across it while studying Descartes's *Meditations*. My initial reaction was one of utter incredulity. How could anyone take such a preposterous argument seriously?

But then I thought about it some more. To my surprise, I found that when I cleared my mind of the notion of God as some kind of ghost or bearded old man, and instead considered God in the abstract, as a being possessed of all perfections, the argument began to make sense. I began to think that Descartes might just be right after all.

It turns out that I was in good company. The English philosopher Bertrand Russell had a similar experience when he was a young man. In his autobiography he wrote: 'I had gone out to buy a tin of tobacco, and was going back with it along Trinity Lane, when I suddenly threw it up in the air and exclaimed: "Great God in Boots! – the ontological argument is sound!"'

Like me, Russell later changed his mind. But it all goes to show the extraordinary hypnotic power of the ontological argument. As Russell was later to observe, it is far easier to say it's no good than it is to work out precisely what's wrong with it.

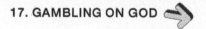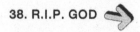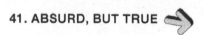

8

THE REAL WORLD

The world around us, the changing world we see, hear, touch, taste and smell, isn't the real world. It is a world of mere shadows and illusion. The real world is timeless and changeless, and can be perceived only by the intellect. This astounding claim was put forward by the Greek thinker Plato (427–347 BC), one of the undisputed giants of philosophy.

Plato's so-called Theory of Forms has been the subject of intense debate and the cause of much bafflement ever since he proposed it. In *The History of Ancient Philosophy from 600 BCE to 500 CE*, Brian Duignan writes: 'Plato is both famous and infamous for his theory of forms. Just what the theory is, and whether it was ever viable, are matters of extreme controversy'.

Clearly, it's not an easy theory either to explain or to grasp. Luckily, in his most famous dialogue, the *Republic*, Plato provides us with a parable, the Analogy of the Cave, to ease us into its complexities and abstractions.

A world of shadows

Imagine a cave, deep underground. Inside is a group of prisoners shackled tightly so that they can see nothing but the wall in front of them. Behind them, and unbeknown to them, their captors are using firelight and puppet-figures to perform shadow-plays on the wall.

The prisoners have spent their entire lives watching shadows and listening to voices that they believe emanate from those shadows. They mistake the shadow-world for reality, and cannot so much as conceive of anything beyond it.

Imagine now that one of the prisoners is unshackled and turned towards the fire. At first he is dazzled and confused. But gradually he begins to realise that the fire, the puppeteers and their puppets are responsible for the shadows he once considered real. Sometime later, he is led out of the cave into the sunlight. Again, he is dazzled at first. But eventually he becomes aware that this is a world more real and more beautiful than the shadowy world he once inhabited. Finally, he is able to gaze upon the sun itself; and to recognise it as the source and sustainer of all things.

The world of Forms

In Plato's parable, the plight of the prisoners represents the human condition. We, like them, are trapped in a world of illusion. In our case, the realm of the senses. We take this to be the real world, not realising that beyond it there lies a world more fully real; a world invisible to the senses but accessible to the intellect; a perfect, unchanging world. The world of the Forms.

But what exactly *are* the Forms? This is a tricky question. There is no simple and unequivocal answer. But we can begin to shed some light on it by considering a specific example: the Form of the Circle.

The sensory world provides us with plenty of examples of circles: the outline of the full moon; the iris of the eye; ripples spreading out across a lake; etc. But none of these is perfectly circular. Careful scrutiny will reveal small bumps, bulges and imperfections; small deviations from absolute circularity.

You might try to draw a circle. But no matter how carefully you construct it, you will never get it quite right. It will never be perfect. There is, however, an ideal Circle; a perfect, eternal and unchanging Circle; a Circle that can be apprehended only by the intellect. This is the Form of the Circle. It exists not in space and time but in the realm of Forms.

Beauty, truth . . . and tables

Beauty also has a Form. There is, in addition to all of the beautiful objects in the sensible world, a Form of Beauty. And just as the Form of the Circle is perfectly circular, so the Form of Beauty is perfectly beautiful.

Perhaps surprisingly, there is also a Form of the Table. The sensible world contains many tables of various shapes and sizes, constructed from a variety of materials. None of these tables lasts forever. They all come into and go out of existence. But the Form of the Table is eternal.

In fact, almost every object and quality has a Form. Circles, squares, triangles, cubes and dodecahedrons have Forms. So do tables, chairs and houses. So, too, do dogs, cats and people. Ditto for beauty, justice, goodness and truth. But Plato harbours doubts about whether undignified objects such as mud, dirt and hair have Forms.

Why Forms?

This is all quite fascinating. But it prompts an obvious question. What were Plato's reasons for postulating the existence of the Forms? What arguments did he produce?

Well, Plato didn't really provide direct proofs so much as intuitive reasons for believing in the Forms. He postulated their existence in order to solve certain philosophical problems, some of which are described below.

Objects of knowledge

The world contains a multitude of beautiful things: beautiful flowers, beautiful people, beautiful vases, beautiful sunsets, beautiful music, etc. What all of these very different things have in common is the quality of *beauty*. There are many beautiful things but only one universal concept of beauty. Plato referred to this as the Form of Beauty, or Beauty itself.

Plato thought that Beauty itself isn't a mere notion but a genuine existent; a real thing. It must be real, he argued, else it could not be an object of thought. If it were not real, we would not be able to grasp it with our intellects.

By Plato's account, each individual beautiful object is beautiful by virtue of the fact that it partakes of, or resembles, Beauty itself. But the precise nature of this participation or resemblance is never spelled out.

Argument from opposites

We often assign properties to items in the world of experience. We say that a certain woman is *beautiful*; two planks of wood are *equal*; a given law is *just*; and so on. But, said Plato, there is always a perspective from which the opposite is true. The woman may be beautiful in comparison to other women but not beautiful in comparison to Aphrodite. The planks may be equal in length but not equal in width. The law may appear just in many respects but unjust in others.

We can never say of anything in the world of experience that it is unqualifiedly beautiful, unqualifiedly equal or unqualifiedly just. Nonetheless we *do* grasp what it means really and truly to be those things. Where does this knowledge come from? By acquaintance with the Forms, said Plato.

It is only because we have innate knowledge of the Forms that we comprehend true beauty, true equality and true justice. It is only through our acquaintance with Beauty itself,

Equality itself and Justice itself that we recognise those properties in the items of everyday experience.

The 'one over many' argument

In the *Republic*, the character Socrates says 'there is one Form for each set of many things to which we give the same name'. Thus there are many beds but only one Form of the Bed; many tables but only one Form of the Table; and so on.

What is it that enables us to apply the name 'bed' to all the individual beds in the world? What's the common property that all beds share? Plato's answer is that beds are beds by virtue of the relationship they bear to the Form of the Bed; by virtue of their common property of Bedness.

It's the Form of the Bed that makes something a bed; the Form of Justice that makes something just; and so on. Similarly, Beautiful things are beautiful because they partake of the Form of Beauty; good things are good because they partake of the Form of Goodness; and so on.

The 'third man' objection

Here, it is worth pointing out that although the theory of Forms is central to Plato's philosophy he never provided a systematic account of it. Instead, there are references to it and discussions of it scattered throughout his works. For Plato, the theory of Forms seems always to have been a work in progress; a good but unfinished idea.

In fact, Plato raised a number of objections to his own theory. The most famous, and perhaps the most damaging, has become known as the *third man argument*. This takes as its starting point Plato's suggestion that Forms are exemplars: that the Form of Beauty is beautiful; the Form of Justice is just; and so on.

If that is the case, then not only is each individual male human being a man, but the Form of Man is also a man. But as we learned previously, 'there is one Form for each set of many things to which we give the same name'. Now, since we give the name 'man' to individual male human beings and also to the Form of Man, there must be some other Form – let's call it Man 2 – in which they both partake. But things don't stop there. Man 2 is also a man, and therefore it must have in common with other men that it partakes in some common Form, Man 3. And so on, and so on, *ad infinitum*.

There is still a lot of debate as to whether Plato considered the third man argument fatal to his Theory of Forms or whether he thought that his theory could be modified to avoid it.

15. ALL IN THE MIND

16. NOW I REMEMBER

36. WORLD 3

9

ORANGES AREN'T ORANGE

I remember, as a child, sitting on the school field one summer's day when a thought struck me. I turned to a friend and said, 'How do I know that the colours *I* see are the same as the colours *you* see?' I explained that although we could both agree that the grass was green and the sky blue, that didn't necessarily mean that we saw those colours the same way. Perhaps my ideas of green and blue were different than his.

That struck me as a pretty strange notion at the time. But I have since learned something even stranger. There are, in fact, good reasons for denying that colours exist at all. At least, not in the sense that we ordinarily take them to exist. These reasons were well understood by the likes of Galileo and Descartes, but were most clearly articulated by the English philosopher John Locke (1632–1704).

Perception

Locke subscribed to the corpuscularian theory of matter, then current, according to which all physical objects are composed of minute particles. According to the corpuscularian theory, the way that objects influence one another is through mechanical interactions between those particles.

To Locke it seemed clear that perception must operate along the same lines. It must involve a causal chain beginning with the motion of the particles in the object perceived, continuing through impact with particles in the sensory organs, and ending with the motion of particles in the brain. Somehow this results in the conscious experiences of seeing, hearing, feeling, tasting and smelling.

Objects in the world, then, operate upon our senses and cause ideas in our minds. These ideas represent physical objects to our consciousness. Consequently we never perceive objects in the world directly, but only indirectly by means of our ideas. When I look at, say, an orange, what I perceive is not the orange itself but rather a mental representation – a sort of inner sign or model – of it.

Primary and secondary qualities

By Locke's account, objects possess various powers (which he called *qualities*) to produce ideas in our minds. For example, an orange possesses qualities like roundness, firmness, orange-ness, sweetness and so on. But here Locke made an important distinction between two kinds of qualities: primary and secondary.

The *primary qualities* of objects include shape, size and motion. These produce ideas in our minds which resemble actual features of the objects themselves. In other words, we not only think of objects as having shape, size and motion, but objects actually *do have* shape, size and motion. 'Therefore they may be called real qualities', Locke wrote, 'because they really exist in objects'.

The *secondary qualities* of objects include colour, taste and smell. What distinguishes them from primary qualities is that they act upon our senses to produce ideas that bear no resemblance to any actual features of the objects themselves. For example, the idea of whiteness that I have in my mind when I look at a snowball isn't to be found in the snowball itself.

Objects do and don't have secondary qualities

This all seems rather confusing. How can Locke have claimed on the one hand that an orange has secondary qualities such as sweetness and orange-ness; and yet have claimed on the other hand that the orange itself is neither sweet nor orange?

His answer is that secondary qualities are not so much features of objects themselves as features of the way objects interact with perceivers. The way a given object looks, tastes and smells ultimately boils down to the manner in which its constituent particles, by virtue of their primary qualities, act upon our sensory apparatus. It is the size, shape and motion of its microscopic particles that causes an orange to look orange, not the supposed orange-ness of the particles themselves.

Locke wrote: '[Secondary qualities] . . . in truth are nothing in the objects themselves, but powers to produce various sensations in us by their primary qualities.' So strictly speaking we oughtn't to say that an orange *is* orange, but rather that it *appears* orange.

He added that if there were no eyes to see, no ears to hear, no noses to smell and no tongues to taste, then all colours, sounds, odours and tastes, as we ordinarily think of them, would vanish and cease, and be reduced to their causes.

Scientific postscript

Science has, of course, moved on since Locke's time. Locke would have said that the idea of orange (the colour) arises in the mind as a result of the interaction of particles from the orange with our eyes. Today we would speak in terms of the way atoms at the surface of the orange are affected by light, and the way in which the light then affects our eyes. But our modern scientific explanation will still be couched in terms of primary rather than secondary qualities.

15. ALL IN THE MIND

28. THE BRAIN IN THE JAR

10

COSMIC COMEUPPANCE

If you're finding life tough, don't complain. You deserve it. According to the law of *karma*, a fundamental principle of Hindu philosophy, your past actions account for your present situation. So if you're suffering now, you must have done some bad stuff in the past.

Everyone else's suffering is fully deserved too. The infant wasting away in a famine-ravaged country is only getting what's coming to him. The old woman who ekes out a miserable existence on the rubbish-heaps of Delhi has no cause to complain. It's all perfectly just and fair. It's all down to karma.

Cosmic comeuppance

Karma, the principle that no suffering or enjoyment can be undeserved, is an astonishing idea. Not least because it seems to be plainly contradicted by the facts. No reasonable person can deny that wicked people sometimes prosper and that good people often suffer.

But the difficulty can be resolved by taking into account another fundamental principle of Hindu philosophy: *samsara*. The Upanishads, an ancient and revered collection of Indian religious and philosophical writings, put forward the idea that after people die they are reborn into new lives. This is the doctrine of samsara, or reincarnation. Taken together, karma and samsara ensure that everyone eventually reaps what they sow.

The accumulation of good karma can result in a birth into a healthy body and a wealthy family. Bad karma can result in birth into a sickly body and a poor family, or even rebirth as an animal.

Philosophical justification

The distinguished Hindu philosopher and former president of India, Radhakrishnan (1888–1975), saw the principles of karma and samsara as essential features of an ordered universe. 'In an ordered world', he said, 'sudden embodiment of conscious life would be meaningless . . . It would be a violation of the rhythm of nature, an effect without a cause, a fragmentary present without a past.'

The idea here is that the very fact that we exist in these particular bodies and with these particular natures confirms the existence of karma and the law of rebirth. How else could we account for our existence? How else could we account for the differences between us? Were it not for karma and samsara these things would be random and meaningless. There would be no reason for us to *be*; and no reason for us to be the way we are.

Radhakrishnan says that karma ought not to be understood in terms of punishment and reward but rather in terms of cause and effect; in terms of actions having their fitting consequences. Not to accept karma and samsara would mean viewing the universe as unjust; but to accept them is to understand that nothing is to blame for the ills and suffering of the world apart from our own actions.

Enlightenment

According to Hindu philosophy, the ultimate aim of human life is *moksha*, or enlightenment. The literal meaning of moksha is 'liberation' or 'setting free'. But what is it that the enlightened person is liberated or set free from? Well, for one thing, from ordinary desires and attachments. The enlightened person grasps the true nature of absolute reality. She achieves a state in which ordinary distinctions such as those between the self and the non-self and the knower and the known disappear. She is able to view the world with detachment, freed from the cares of ordinary existence.

Moksha is also liberation from samsara; from the cycle of births and deaths. How does this work? Well, samsara is fuelled by karma. Good actions produce good karma which inevitably leads to good fortune; bad actions produce bad karma which inevitably leads to bad fortune. So the karma accumulated in one life must be, as it were, expended in future ones.

But according to the Hindu religious text, the *Bhagavad Gita*, desireless action (action unmotivated by hatred, greed or desire) does not result in karma. So the enlightened person does not accrue karma, and is released from samsara.

Karma's dark side

The concept of karma originated in the religion and philosophy of ancient India. But in recent times it has become quite a widespread and popular belief. People the world over are drawn to the idea that cosmic justice prevails and that people ultimately get what they deserve. Also, people find it comforting to think that even though the present life may have been marred by mistakes and disappointments, there will be other chances further down the line.

But although many people view karma as a comforting and just principle, critics point out that it has its dark side. The idea that people get what they deserve is all very well in the abstract. But when applied to specific cases, it can seem callous in the extreme. How many of those who draw consolation from the idea of karma would be willing to say that sick people deserve to be sick? Or that starving children deserve to starve?

Furthermore, belief in karma can make people accepting of

social injustice. In traditional Hindu society, people often accept that the manner of their birth and their role within the caste system are determined by karma built up in previous lives. And they will often seek to avoid building up bad karma for future lives by acting in accordance with the rules laid down for people of their station.

Those born into the higher castes may regard themselves as meriting their privileges. Those born into the lowest caste may regard themselves as deserving their low status, and as being duty-bound to serve those of a higher caste by doing the most degrading and poorly paid jobs.

23. AN END TO SUFFERING

26. ONE HAND CLAPPING

11

IT'S ALL IN THE NUMBERS

What is the world made from? Modern readers, depending upon their level of scientific knowledge, are likely to answer that the world is made from atoms; or from protons, neutrons and electrons; or from quarks, photons, neutrinos and suchlike.

Many early philosophers asked themselves the same question. Thales of Miletus (624–546 BC) considered the matter carefully and decided that everything is water. Anaximenes (585–525 BC) identified the fundamental substance as air. Democritus (460–370 BC) said that everything is made from indivisible, imperishable atoms. But perhaps the most bizarre-sounding theory came from Pythagoras (c.550–c.500 BC) who said that everything is number.

This is a bizarre claim. After all, numbers are insubstantial. They lack physical existence. So how can the world *be* numbers? How can numbers *make* anything?

These aren't easy questions to answer. There are no surviving writings of Pythagoras, and his disciples were all sworn to secrecy about his ideas and beliefs. So we only learn about his doctrines second-hand, and in rather sketchy detail, from later thinkers such as Aristotle.

This leaves a big question mark over precisely what Pythagoras meant when he said that everything is number. But there are two plausible answers. One has to do with the relationship between numbers and shapes; and the other has to do with number-patterns in nature.

Numbers and shapes

Pythagoras and his disciples were interested in both arithmetic and geometry, and they linked the two together in a way that seems curious to us today. They viewed numbers in spatial terms. Numbers like 1, 4, 9, 16, etc. they termed *square* numbers because they can be represented by dots or pebbles laid out in the shape of a square. For similar reasons, they described 2, 6, 12, 20, 30, etc. as *oblong* numbers; 1, 3, 6, 10, 15, etc. as *triangular* numbers; and so on. Additionally, they thought of the number one as a point; the number two as a line; the number three as a surface; and the number four as a solid (since you can build a three-dimensional pyramid out of four pebbles).

If we think of the objects in nature in spatial terms, as defined by points, lines and surfaces, we can perhaps gain an inkling of what it might mean to claim that everything is number.

Numbers in nature

One of the Pythagoreans' most important and ground-breaking discoveries was the link between music and mathematics. According to some stories, Pythagoras made this discovery while experimenting with a single-stringed instrument called a monochord. He found that when the open string of the monochord was plucked it produced a note of a certain pitch, and that when the length of the string was halved it produced a note an octave higher.

Further investigation revealed that strings whose lengths are in the ratio 2:1 produce the musical interval of an octave; strings in the ratio 3:2 produce an interval of a perfect fifth; strings in the ratio 4:3 produce a perfect fourth; and so on. It turns out that all musical notes that harmonise nicely together are connected by neat mathematical relationships like these.

The fact that mathematics and musical harmony are linked must have been an amazing revelation. It certainly got the Pythagoreans fired up, and set them thinking that perhaps there are mathematical ratios at the heart of *everything*. Perhaps all natural phenomena, as well as qualities like beauty, goodness and truth, are grounded in number.

So far as the natural world is concerned, this insight has proved immensely fruitful. The idea that physical phenomena and the relationships between them can be expressed mathematically lies at the very heart of science. But Pythagorean ideas concerning the numerical basis of qualities like goodness, truth and justice have not withstood the test of time so well. Their ideas on this subject now seem arbitrary and fanciful.

For example, they viewed odd numbers as masculine and even numbers as feminine (the number one was considered both odd and even). Accordingly, the number five, being comprised of the first masculine and the first feminine number, was assigned to marriage. For reasons no more compelling or convincing, four was considered the number of justice; six the number of creation; ten the number of the universe; and so on.

Everything is number

The Pythagoreans, then, saw number in everything: in the shapes and properties of physical objects; in qualities such as beauty and justice; and in concepts like marriage and creation. Small wonder, then, that they came to view number as fundamental; as being somehow the grounding of all things. Thus we arrive at a plausible interpretation – or, at least, the hint of a plausible interpretation – of the claim that everything is number.

More Pythagorean weirdness

'Everything is number' wasn't Pythagoras' only strange idea. Not by a long shot. He, perhaps more than any other philosopher, exemplifies the notion of the crackpot genius.

As well as being a philosopher, a mathematician and a scientist, Pythagoras was the founder of a religious and scholarly community. He was a strict disciplinarian, and gave lots of edicts to his disciples. For example, they weren't allowed to pick up anything that had fallen over, sleep at noon, urinate facing the sun, step across a pole or write in the snow. Most famously, they were forbidden from eating beans.

According to one legend, Pythagoras' bean-avoiding obsession led to his death. He was running away from some enemies but came to a dead stop when he reached the edge of a beanfield. His persecutors caught up with him and slit his throat.

12

DAN BROWN VS SHAKESPEARE

When someone asks me what my favourite film is, I answer, without hesitation, *The Karate Kid* (Part I). At this point, my wife generally accuses me of affectation. She's convinced I harbour a secret preference for *Schindler's List*, *Gandhi* or *Citizen Kane*.

What makes her think I really prefer *Citizen Kane*? I'm not entirely sure. But it has something to do with it being 'better' than *The Karate Kid*, in the same way that Puccini is 'better' than the Pussycat Dolls, and Shakespeare is 'better' than Dan Brown. She credits me, I think, with more refined taste than I possess.

But is Puccini *really* better than the Pussycat Dolls? Is Shakespeare *really* superior to Dan Brown? And is it *really* poor taste to prefer *The Karate Kid* to *Citizen Kane*? Not according to the English philosopher Jeremy Bentham, it isn't. For him, all talk of good and bad taste was pure hogwash.

Jeremy Bentham, happiness calculator

Jeremy Bentham was born in 1748 into a prosperous middle-class family. As a child he was painfully shy and nervous but possessed of a remarkable intelligence. He began to study Latin at the age of four, and entered Oxford University at the age of twelve.

After graduating, he studied law. He qualified, but did not practise. Instead he devoted his considerable energy and talent to thinking and writing about legal reform. In 1789 he published his masterwork, *An Introduction to the Principles of Morals and Legislation*.

Bentham was a *hedonist*. He equated happiness with pleasure, and believed that a happy life is simply one in which pleasure outweighs pain. His hedonist principles led him to formulate an ethical doctrine known as utilitarianism which holds that something is 'good' only insofar as it maximises pleasure or minimises pain.

A central feature of Bentham's utilitarianism is the 'Greatest Happiness Principle', according to which the morally correct action in any situation is the one that brings the greatest happiness to the greatest number of people. This principle is foundational to all of Bentham's ideas about legal and social reform.

It's very difficult, of course, to judge the effect that one's actions might have on the overall happiness of the community. Bentham realised this, and so came up with a *felicific calculus*: a method of calculating the amount of pleasure and pain that actions are likely to cause. The felicific calculus is too complex and time-consuming to be used by individuals. Bentham's idea was that political leaders would use it to help them formulate laws that maximise the happiness of the populace.

So how does all this relate to the issue of good and bad taste?

Push-pin and poetry

In *The Rationale of Reward*, Bentham spoke scathingly of those who decry popular entertainments; who spoil innocent enjoyments by attaching to them 'the fantastic idea of bad taste'; and who consider themselves 'benefactors to the human race' but are really only 'interrupters of their pleasure'.

According to him, when it comes to calculating happiness there are no high-quality or low-quality pleasures. Intense pleasures count for more than mild ones; prolonged pleasures count for more than short-lived ones; and so on. But this is all a matter of degree rather than quality. No pleasure is intrinsically superior to any other.

By this account, the sole criterion for judging the worth of a novel, a play, a piece of music or a pastime is the amount of pleasure it produces. Bentham wrote: 'The utility of all these arts and sciences – I speak both of those of amusement and curiosity – the value which they possess, is exactly in proportion to the pleasure they yield.' He famously declared that push-pin (a child's game, played with pins) is every bit as valuable as music and poetry.

Dan Brown or Shakespeare?

So which is best – which brings more pleasure – Dan Brown or Shakespeare? Well, insofar as individuals are concerned it's a matter of taste. Those who enjoy light reads, fast-paced plots and plenty of twists and turns will get their kicks from *The Da Vinci Code*; while those with a penchant for poetry and psychological insight will find themselves enraptured by *Hamlet*.

But which brings most pleasure *overall*? Dan Brown, no contest. Here's why. Almost everyone who reads Dan Brown does so purely for enjoyment, which amounts to millions of book-sized units of pleasure. Meanwhile, Shakespeare is suffered and endured every bit as often as he is savoured and enjoyed. The Bard gives quite as much pain as pleasure. Therefore, by Bentham's account, Dan Brown is better than Shakespeare.

Not so, says J. S. Mill

Perhaps the most powerful criticism of Bentham's all-pleasures-count-equally claim came from his erstwhile disciple, John Stuart Mill (1806–1873).

Mill's father was a friend and admirer of Bentham, and brought up his son to be a torchbearer for utilitarianism. John Stuart learned his lessons well. He became a keen advocate of Bentham's principles. But at the age of twenty he underwent a 'crisis in [his] mental history'. He stopped deriving any pleasure from his studies; the company of friends left him cold and indifferent; and even his ambition to become a great social reformer ceased to motivate him.

The depression lasted six months. During that time, Bentham's principles did little to comfort and console him. In fact, it was poetry – the poetry of William Wordsworth – that finally provided the much-needed 'medicine for [his] state of mind'.

This experience completely altered Mill's views. It convinced him that some pleasures *are* more valuable than others. No amount of push-pin could have delivered him from depression the way that Wordsworth's poetry had. Bentham had got it wrong. There was more to pleasure than mere quantity. Quality was important too.

Accordingly he separated pleasures into 'lower' and 'higher' ones. The lower ones, such as eating, drinking and sex, can be enjoyed by animals and humans alike. But the higher ones, such as friendship, honour, art, music and poetry, rely on our distinctly human capacities. A life spent in pursuit of exclusively lower-grade pleasures is, in Mill's estimation, a piggy life. It qualifies as a happy one if you happen to be a pig, but it falls far short if you happen to be a person.

There seems little doubt that Mill would have rated Shakespeare more highly than Dan Brown.

 1. NOT *BAD*. JUST MISGUIDED

21. OUCH! I FEEL GOOD

13

BURN, BABY, BURN

St Augustine of Hippo (354–430 AD) is one the best-known figures in the history of the Catholic Church. His accomplishments were dazzling. He was a bishop, a theologian and a rhetorician; he penned one of the most celebrated autobiographies ever written; and he is one of the most influential thinkers of all time.

In philosophy, he made important contributions to our understanding of time, free will, the role and limitations of language, the concept of self, and much more besides. He also said that babies are sinful and deserve to go to Hell.

Sex life of a saint

Like many people, St Augustine was obsessed with sex. As a young man, he took a practical interest in it. He had two concubines (not at the same time), the first of whom bore him a son. During this period of life he uttered his famous prayer: 'Grant me chastity and continence, but not yet.'

Following his conversion, in 386 AD, Augustine opted for a life of celibacy. From then on his interest in sex became purely intellectual. He thought deeply about the theology, philosophy and psychology of sex and came to the conclusion that it is really rather naughty. He saw sexual desire as a dangerous passion that undermines self-control, overrides rational thought and leads to wrong behaviours.

This discussion of Augustine's sex life may seem gratuitous. But his claim that babies deserve Hell cannot be properly understood without first understanding something of his attitude towards sex. Equally, we must come to grips with the notion of original sin. This theological doctrine didn't originate with Augustine, but his ideas about it dominated the teaching of the Western Church for many centuries.

Original sin

The doctrine of original sin basically says that humans are born sinful. We emerge from the womb infected, as it were, with the disease of sin. As a result, we live our lives estranged from God and plagued by evil desires.

Our first parents, Adam and Eve, were created free from sin. But then they ate the forbidden fruit and sin entered and corrupted them. Even worse, they passed on their sinfulness to their children; who, in turn, passed it onto *their* children; and so on; and so on. The net result is that we are all born bad; corrupted by original sin.

Nowadays, of course, many Christian theologians and believers view the story of the Fall as an allegory; a fable in which the characters and events are to be understood as representing spiritual and moral truths. But in Augustine's time the story was taken quite literally. Adam was considered a historical person.

A sexually transmitted disease

How is original sin passed on from one generation to the next? Well, different people have different ideas about this. But Augustine had very clear views on the matter. He taught that original sin is transmitted through sexual intercourse.

Every sexual act, he maintained, contains an element of *concupiscence*: a theological term that he used to denote wrong and lustful desire. Even sex within marriage is tainted by concupiscence, and this wrongful element in sex is the vehicle by which original sin is passed on from father to child.

In his treatise, *De Bono Coniugali* (The Good of Marriage), Augustine wrote: 'Whenever it comes to the actual process of generation, the very embrace which is lawful and honourable cannot be effected without the ardour of lust. . . . Now from this concupiscence whatever comes into being by natural birth is bound by original sin.'

Inherited guilt

One of the gravest consequences of original sin is that it makes us unfit for heaven and deserving of Hell. The only way we can avoid damnation is to place our trust in the redemptive power of Christ and be baptised. This leaves unbaptised babies in an unenviable position. They fulfil neither of the requirements for salvation and must therefore suffer in Hell.

This seems unfair. Surely it is unjust on God's part to consign tiny babies who have committed no actual sins to Hell. Not so, said Augustine. We have to appreciate that there are two aspects to original sin. When we are conceived we inherit not only the spiritual sickness resulting from Adam's fall, but also the guilt associated with his crime. He wrote: 'In the first man all are understood to have sinned, because all were in him when he sinned; . . . it is manifest that in Adam all sinned, so to speak, *en masse.*'

So even tiny newborn babies bear the guilt of sin. Therefore infants whose souls are not cleansed by the waters of baptism must bear their punishment, and God is justified in sending them to Hell.

Augustine: philosopher and theologian

The claim that unbaptised babies will go to Hell is, of course, deeply shocking. Bishop Julian of Eclanum, a contemporary of Augustine who rejected the doctrine of original sin, said that the idea was monstrous. How could God consign babies to Hell merely because Adam ate an apple?

Augustine was sensitive to this point, and was willing to grant that the sufferings of Hell must be extremely mild for unbaptised infants. We might wonder, then, why he held to the doctrine at all. The answer is that he was forced into it by his theological assumptions.

Augustine viewed philosophy as an ally of Christianity; as a means of understanding rather than refuting the Church's doctrines. One of those doctrines was that babies need to be baptised 'for the remission of sins'. But babies haven't committed any personal sins. So what sins are they being baptised *for*? It must be, Augustine reasoned, that they somehow share in the sins of Adam. Otherwise the doctrine of infant baptism doesn't make sense.

Augustine's philosophy was always tightly constrained by his religious beliefs and by the necessity of agreeing with scripture. This can make many of his ideas seem irrelevant and even absurd to those who do not share his theological assumptions. Yet he was, for all that, an exceptionally able thinker who came up with some very profound ideas when engaged in pure philosophy.

A glimmer of hope

Augustine's views on the fate of unbaptised babies held sway in the Catholic Church right up to the thirteenth century. But then a French philosopher and theologian, Peter Abelard, called the doctrine into question. He said that unbaptised infants who have committed no personal sins cannot deserve punishment, and suggested that instead of going to Hell they would go to Limbo: a place where they would experience neither the pains of Hell nor the joys of Heaven. This idea was accepted by Pope Innocent III.

In 2007, prospects for unbaptised babies improved still further. Pope Benedict XVI approved the findings of a report by the International Theological Commission which found 'reasons to hope that infants who die without baptism may be saved and brought into eternal happiness'.

38. R.I.P. GOD

39. THE ULTIMATE VICE

14

AGAIN, AND AGAIN, AND AGAIN . . .

Eternal recurrence, or eternal return, is the theory that history repeats itself, right down to the tiniest detail, infinitely many times. Everything that is happening now has happened countless times already and will happen again countless times in the future.

You have read this chapter innumerable times before. On each occasion, the same thoughts passed through your mind; the same sounds filtered in from outside; and every*one* else and every*thing* else was just as it is now; and just as it will be innumerable times again . . .

Dodgy science?

The doctrine of eternal recurrence is said to have originated in the sixth century BC with the Greek philosopher Pythagoras, and was later taken up by the Stoics. But it found its most powerful expression with the nineteenth-century thinker Friedrich Nietzsche. But what could be the justification for such an outlandish theory?

Well, the argument runs something like this. The universe contains a finite amount of stuff spread out over a finite amount of space. This means that there are only so many possible arrangements of all that stuff. Time, on the other hand, is infinite. Therefore identical arrangements of stuff must eventually recur – and will do so infinitely many times.

The science is, perhaps, a bit ropy. Debatable, to say the least. Modern-day cosmologists are by no means certain that the universe *is* finite. Furthermore, the fundamental particles of modern physics lack the stability and permanence that seem to be required for eternal return. No matter. It is very unlikely that Nietzsche considered eternal recurrence primarily a cosmological theory, and it is his take on it that we will consider here. So we won't fret too much about that aspect of it either.

Psychological testing

What, then, *is* Nietzsche's take on eternal recurrence? That's not an easy question to answer. Nietzsche's ideas are notoriously difficult to pin down, and this one is no exception. But perhaps the most widely held view is that he saw eternal recurrence as a kind of psychological test: a tool for assessing one's strength of mind and attitude towards life.

This seems very plausible. In my experience, Nietzsche's power lies chiefly in his ability to challenge and provoke us; to kick us out of our complacency. So let's lay aside any scientific reservations we might have and consider the doctrine of eternal recurrence in this light. What would its implications be – on a purely personal level – if it *were* true?

In his 1882 work, *The Gay Science*, Nietzsche proposes a thought-experiment. He asks us to imagine that one day or night a demon comes to us 'in our loneliest loneliness' and says:

> This life as you now live it and have lived it, you will have to
> live once more and innumerable times more; and there will
> be nothing new in it, but every pain, every joy and every
> thought and sigh and everything unutterably small or great in
> your life will have to return to you, all in the same succession
> and sequence.

What then? Would the thought of forever repeating every bit of our lives – every dreary, unfulfilled moment; every humiliating defeat; every inconsequential accomplishment – fill us with despair? Or do we value our lives and achievements so highly that we would exult at the prospect?

Crushed or transformed?

Nietzsche thought that the majority of us would throw ourselves down and 'gnash our teeth' at the demon's words. The thought of infinitely multiplying our hardships and miseries, and eternally reliving our dull, meaningless lives, would be more than we could bear.

Only a select few, only the greatest and noblest among us could rejoice and say, in Nietzsche's words, 'You are a god and never have I heard anything more divine!' Why so? Because only the higher human types – only those who live robustly, eschew self-pity and act upon their highest ideals – can embrace life in its entirety.

In his 1888 work, *Ecce Homo*, Nietzsche wrote: 'My formula for greatness in a human being is *amor fati*: that one wants nothing to be different, not forward, not backward, not in all eternity. Not merely bear what is necessary, still less conceal it . . . but *love* it.' (*Amor fati* is a Latin phrase meaning 'love of fate'. Nietzsche used it to refer to an attitude of mind in which one is willing to embrace and affirm the whole of one's life, including its sufferings and disappointments.)

The doctrine of eternal recurrence challenges us to take a long, hard look at our lives and consider whether we would be willing to live them over and over again. If we enter fully into the spirit of the test, according to Nietzsche we will either be crushed or transformed.

Over to you

For some, Nietzsche's challenge really does prove life-transforming. For example, in *Living With Nietzsche*, writer Robert C. Solomon recounts how, as a young man, it inspired him to take a close look at his life and his role in the world. The net result was that he left medical school and devoted himself to philosophy.

As for myself, Nietzsche's challenge leaves me cold. I can't work up any emotional response to the prospect of past and future lives that are unconnected to this one by memory. As far as I'm concerned, if I can't remember it, it wasn't me.

But forget Solomon and myself. With Nietzsche, the important thing is to apply his ideas to your own life. So try it. 'The eternal hourglass of existence is turned upside down again and again, and you with it, speck of dust!' Are you dismayed? Inspired? Or couldn't you care less?

38. R.I.P. GOD ➥

43. THE UNEXAMINED LIFE ➥

15

ALL IN THE MIND

The Irish philosopher George Berkeley (1685–1753) is best known for his astonishing claim that there is no such thing as matter; that minds and ideas exist and nothing else.

To most of us, it seems obvious that the world contains material objects that exist whether anyone is observing them or not. But according to Berkeley we are mistaken. He said that so-called material objects are really just collections of ideas and cannot exist independently of minds.

Consider, for example, a pebble lying on a beach. What can we say about it? It is grey and round; it is hard and smooth; it feels heavy when we lift it; it smells vaguely of sea-water and tastes a bit salty. But all of these descriptions merely report our own perceptions; our own *ideas*.

We assume that these ideas are caused by a material object which by virtue of its physical properties stimulates our sense organs, which in turn send signals to our brains, and so on. But Berkeley did not agree. According to him, the pebble *is* the ideas of greyness, hardness, saltiness, etc.; nothing more.

Berkeley's philosophy, and any other philosophy that holds that the world is ultimately mental, is known as *idealism*. The contrasting doctrine, that only matter exists, is known as *materialism*.

The source of our ideas

If the ideas that represent the world to us are not caused by material objects, then what *are* they caused by? Berkeley's answer is God. All of the visual, auditory, tactile, gustatory and olfactory experiences that represent to us the world and its objects are placed into our minds directly by God.

When I direct my gaze towards a pebble, God implants certain colours and shapes in my mind. When I kick the pebble, God implants certain tactile ideas in my mind and alters my visual impressions consistent with the pebble skidding along the beach. When you direct your gaze towards the same pebble, God implants ideas in your mind too. These are consistent with the behaviour of the pebble from your viewpoint.

A consequence of this account of reality is that there are no unperceived objects. If a pebble isn't being looked at, felt, smelled, tasted, listened to or in some other way perceived then it is no pebble at all. It doesn't exist. Does this mean that objects are continually popping into and out of existence? Not at all, said Berkeley, because all of the objects in nature reside constantly in the mind of God. They are perceived by Him, if no one else.

Heads, shoulders, knees and toes

Even our own bodies are collections of ideas. We have hands, feet, brains, ears, eyes, a nervous system and so forth. But what 'having ears' means is that when I look in a mirror, God will implant ear-shaped visual impressions in my mind; when I cover my ears, God will dull my auditory impressions; and so on. This is a very odd notion. It means that not only are the things we see, feel and hear bundles of ideas, but so are the things we see, feel and hear with.

Nothing is real?

Reality, then, consists of minds and ideas. Nothing else. Does this mean that nothing is real? That rocks, stars, clouds and trees are mere illusions? Not at all. The world according to Berkeley looks, feels, tastes, smells and sounds identical to the world of the materialist. The objects in Berkeley's world behave just as consistently and just as predictably as those in the materialist's. The only thing missing from Berkeley's world is *matter* – and this, Berkeley argued, is a redundant notion anyway.

Idealism vs. materialism

Berkeley's idealism may sound crazy, but that doesn't necessarily mean it's wrong. Think of it this way. There are two competing accounts of reality: the materialist's world of material objects; and Berkeley's world of objects that are nothing more than collections of ideas. Both worlds look, sound, feel, taste and smell the same. There's no experimental test you can perform that will show you which theory is correct. All you can do is ask yourself which is most plausible.

There is no doubt that the idealist's world strikes us as odd. But Berkeley countered that the materialist's world is odder still since it is composed of something we can neither know nor understand, and which close analysis reveals to be downright impossible. Namely matter.

What's the matter with matter?

Berkeley employed a number of arguments to convince us that materialism is false. One of these aims to show that matter is inconceivable. Consider, again, a pebble. It appears to be a certain shape, size and colour; it feels hard and smooth; and so on. These are all sensory impressions, or, in Berkeley's terminology, *ideas*. Subtract these from your concept of the pebble and what remains? Nothing. You can't form any notion of the material substance that is supposed to underpin them. Matter is, then, inconceivable. Sure, we can use words like 'matter', 'material object' and suchlike. But they are empty; meaningless.

Another of Berkeley's arguments aims to convince us that matter is superfluous. The materialist philosophers of Berkeley's time were committed to a world-view in which God creates physical objects that operate upon our senses to create ideas in our minds. But this makes matter redundant. It is neater and simpler, said Berkeley, to take matter out of the equation and have God place sensory impressions directly in our minds. (We, of course, may be less willing than Berkeley's contemporaries to accept the God-assumption upon which this argument depends).

But Berkeley's favourite argument, which he considered a knock-down blow to materialism, is the so-called Master Argument. He used it to try to convince us that matter is impossible; that the very notion of mind-independent matter is contradictory.

In claiming to conceive of matter, Berkeley argued, the materialist claims to conceive of that which exists unperceived. But this is just as absurd as claiming to *see* that which is *unseen*. It's true that we might picture in our minds a book or a tree existing unperceived, but in doing so we are thinking of, or perceiving, that very book or tree!

To this, the materialist may counter that, admittedly, when she thinks of a tree the *thought of a tree* is in her mind. But this is not at all to say that the *tree itself* is in her mind. Sure, the *idea* is in her mind; but the thing that the idea is *of* is outside her mind.

Crazy, but perhaps not so crazy

Berkeley's anti-materialist arguments may seem strange, even silly. But it can be surprisingly difficult to pinpoint precisely what's wrong with them. Few philosophers have ultimately been convinced by Berkeley's claim that matter is impossible. But many, including David Hume and Immanuel Kant, have felt the full force of his arguments to the effect that matter is inconceivable; that we use the term without having the faintest idea what we mean by it.

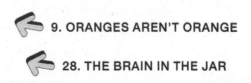

9. ORANGES AREN'T ORANGE

28. THE BRAIN IN THE JAR

16

NOW I REMEMBER

Every schoolchild knows Pythagoras' Theorem: that in a right-angled triangle the square of the hypotenuse is equal to the sum of the squares of the other two sides. I remember memorising and using it when I was twelve years old. But it wasn't until I was about fifteen that I followed through a proof of the theorem and can be said to have really understood it.

So how long have I known Pythagoras' Theorem? Since I memorised it, aged twelve? Or since I understood it, aged fifteen? In Plato's view, neither answer is correct. According to him, I have *always* known it. I learned it long before I was born. All that happened in my maths lessons was that my teachers gave my memory a nudge, enabling me to recollect what I already knew.

What reasons did Plato have for making this extraordinary claim? Well, he provided two main arguments. One can be found in the *Meno* and the other in the *Phaedo*. Let's begin with the *Meno*.

Socrates teaches geometry

The *Meno* is a dialogue in which two main speakers, the philosopher Socrates and a well-educated young man named Meno, discuss human virtue. One of its most interesting features is a practical demonstration by Socrates of the idea that what we call learning is really remembering.

Socrates calls over one of Meno's slave-boys and presents him with a geometrical problem. He draws a square measuring two feet by two feet, and gets the boy to agree that its area is four square feet. Socrates then asks how long each side would need to be to make a square twice as big.

Without hesitation, the boy replies that in order to double the area of the square it would be necessary to double the lengths of its sides. The answer therefore is that each side would need to be four feet long.

Socrates then leads the boy, by a process of skilful questioning, to realise that his answer, though seemingly obvious, is wrong. Thence follows a fascinating account of how Socrates leads the boy, little by little, to discover the correct answer for himself. (The side of the larger square must equal the diagonal of the original one.)

'Watch out in case you ever find me teaching and instructing him instead of drawing out his own opinions', Socrates instructs Meno. Meno watches carefully and bears witness to the fact that Socrates never engages in any direct teaching.

Since the slave-boy arrives at the correct answer for himself, Socrates concludes that he must have already had the appropriate knowledge inside of him. Rather than learning anything new, he has merely been prompted to recollect knowledge he already had.

The immortality of the soul

Plato's learning-is-remembering doctrine is related to his belief in the immortality of the soul. In the *Meno*, Socrates says that the soul of man is immortal and is repeatedly incarnated. This accounts for the vast store of innate knowledge inside every one of us. Each human soul has been born and reborn many times before. It has seen everything, both in this world and in the world of Forms. 'There is nothing it has not [already] learned.'

A proof from the *Phaedo*

Plato's second justification for his learning-is-remembering theory comes from the *Phaedo* and runs like this. When we look at a picture of someone, we recollect the person themselves, and can judge how closely the image resembles them. By the same process, when we observe two 'equal' pieces of wood we are able to see that they fall short of the abstract property of equality (since no two pieces of wood are precisely the same length).

But where did we acquire the abstract notion of equality if not through the senses? Clearly, we must have acquired it – along with knowledge of other abstract essences such as goodness, truth and beauty – before we were born. The soul previously existed in the world of Forms. There it gazed upon Equality Itself, Goodness Itself, Truth Itself and Beauty Itself, etc. Skilful questioning can prompt the soul to recollect these things.

A simple objection

I mentioned Socrates' geometry lesson to my wife, Wendy, who teaches in a primary school. She was impressed by the pedagogy but not the philosophy. 'I don't see that it proves learning is remembering', she said. 'It just shows that people have the ability to work things out.'

Wendy may not be a philosopher, but I think she hit the nail on the head. Plato convinces us that there's a gap – a very impressive gap – between what Socrates teaches and what the pupil learns. But the learning-is-remembering theory doesn't seem to be the most plausible way to fill it. An inbuilt capacity for rational thought seems a less fanciful alternative (though, of course, this leads us to wonder about the source of this innate capacity).

Credit to Plato, though, for raising such important questions about the nature of teaching and learning.

 **8. THE REAL WORLD**

17

GAMBLING ON GOD

You ought to believe in God even if you don't think He exists. That's the startling conclusion to the so-called wager argument which was devised by the French mathematician, scientist and theologian Blaise Pascal (1623–62).

Pascal and probability

Pascal was a pioneer of probability theory: a branch of mathematics concerned with the analysis of random events. In 1654, he and Pierre de Fermat exchanged letters discussing mathematical problems associated with games of chance. From this collaboration, probability theory was born. In the wager argument, Pascal applied the mathematics of probability to the thorny question of whether we ought or ought not to believe in God.

Pascal's wager

The argument appears in Pascal's notes for the *Pensées*, a proposed book defending the Christian faith. Sadly, Pascal died before completing it, and so his celebrated argument has had to be pieced together from some rather disordered jottings. It runs something like this.

Either God exists or He doesn't. Despite your best endeavours you can't work out which. So which way should you incline: towards belief or unbelief? Well, since reason cannot decide you must take a gamble. Heads or tails? But before you call you ought to consider the risks and rewards. What do you stand to gain or lose if you bet on God? And what do you stand to gain or lose if you bet against Him?

First, consider the potential gains and losses of choosing to believe. In that case, if God exists you get to enjoy eternal bliss, and if He doesn't exist you will perhaps lose out on some worldly pleasures. So you may gain an infinite reward or you may lose a finite one.

Next, consider the potential gains and losses of choosing not to believe. In that case, if God exists you will lose out on eternal bliss, and if He doesn't exist you stand to gain very little. So the best you can hope for is a finite gain.

Recapping: the potential gain associated with believing is infinite whereas the potential gain associated with not believing is finite. The choice, then, is a no-brainer. You ought to believe.

Doubt God? Believe anyway

Pascal intended to address his wager to those genuinely in two minds about whether or not to believe. The *Pensées* was supposed to bring the reader to precisely this point. Interestingly, though, the argument seems to demonstrate the prudence of believing in God even if you doubt His existence. Here's why.

Even if you think the chances that God exists are a thousand to one, believing in Him is still your best bet. The expected value of believing equals the probability that God exists multiplied by the reward you'll receive if your gamble on Him pays off. But a thousand to one times infinity equals infinity. So the expected value of believing is infinite.

The same holds true even if you think there's a million-to-one chance, or even a billion-to-one chance, that God exists. No matter how unlikely you think it is that God exists, the maths says you ought to believe in Him anyway.

Some versions of the wager argument introduce an extra element into the calculations: namely, the eternal punishment of non-believers. This packs a huge psychological punch. After all, who wants to risk spending eternity in torment?

Not so fast, Monsieur Pascal!

Pascal's wager is open to a number of objections. For one thing, beliefs don't seem to be the kind of things we can adopt at will. It seems wrong to say that we can choose to believe in God.

Pascal's response is that although we can't simply decide to believe, we can, if we choose, put ourselves in the way of belief by attending Masses, praying, reading the Bible and so forth. If we persevere in these outward acts of faith, Pascal thinks that we will eventually acquire a genuine and sincere belief.

Another problem with the wager argument is that it seems to apply not only to belief in the Christian God, but to belief in any deity who offers infinite rewards. How then are we to choose between competing religions?

In addition, in matters of religion it seems inappropriate to base one's beliefs on self-interested calculations. Heartfelt faith seems more the ticket.

A sensible suggestion

It's all a bit of a headache. So perhaps the best response to the wager is to forget all about it and go have a beer. Why so? Because this strategy has an infinite expected value – and comes with a beer.

Here's the calculation. If you go have a beer there is always a chance, however slight, that you will have a Damascus experience and come to believe in God. Let's say the chances of that happening are a million to one. In that case, the expected value of having a beer is one-millionth of the expected value of simply deciding to believe. But that makes the expected value one-millionth of infinity, i.e. infinite. Cheers!

 **7. TOTAL PERFECTION**

38. R.I.P. GOD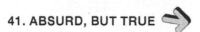

41. ABSURD, BUT TRUE

18

THE GHOST IN THE MACHINE

The French philosopher René Descartes was a *dualist*. He held that the universe contains two kinds of substance: matter and mind. The essential property of matter is that it is extended (it takes up space) whereas the essential property of mind is that it thinks.

A human being, according to Descartes, consists of an immaterial mind united somehow to a material body. The mind is the bit of us that does the thinking, feeling, desiring, perceiving and so on. The body is the bit of us that does the moving around.

The ghost in the machine

This is a strange notion. It conjures up an image of some kind of ethereal entity floating around inside the body; of a 'ghost in the machine'.

Close inspection reveals Descartes's mind/body theory to be even weirder than it first appears. Bodies, according to this theory, are material objects. They have shapes and sizes and are located in space; but they do not think. Minds, on other hand, *do* think; but they have neither shape nor size and are not located in space.

It's easy to understand why Descartes supposed that bodies do not think. Few people believe that material objects like stones, clouds or atoms think. And few people find it conceivable that an object consisting solely of material parts, however complex its structure, can have thoughts, feeling and ideas.

But what made Descartes think that minds are not located in space? Well, although he could pretend or imagine that he had no body, he could not pretend or imagine that he had no mind (the very act of pretending or imagining presupposes a mind). This convinced him that his mind was the most essential part of himself; that it could exist without his body; and that it 'had no need for any place to exist'.

The union of the mind and body is, by this account, of a very curious sort because the mind isn't where the body is. In fact, the mind isn't *anywhere*. The ghost in the machine isn't *in* the machine!

The mind-body problem

This brings us to one of the most fiercely debated, most intractable problems, in the history of philosophy: the mind-body problem.

If, as Descartes claimed, mind and body are two distinct substances then how can they possibly interact? How can mental events such as thoughts, feelings and desires give rise to bodily actions? And how can bodily processes give rise to thoughts, feelings and desires?

That mental events cause physical ones, and that physical events cause mental ones, seems beyond reasonable doubt. I form the intention to walk and my legs start moving. I touch the surface of a hot iron and I feel intense pain. But how can this be? How can a thought set matter in motion? And how can a physical interaction generate a feeling?

Princess Elisabeth of Bohemia, who corresponded regularly with Descartes on philosophical matters, asked the great man these very questions. But he was unable to give her a satisfactory answer. He was convinced that the interaction between mind and body occurs in the brain, specifically in the pineal gland, a pine-cone-shaped organ located between the two hemispheres. But he had nothing very substantial or convincing to say about *how* the interaction occurs. Furthermore, it is difficult to make sense of his claim that mind/body interaction occurs in the brain given his conviction that minds are not located in space.

The mind-body problem has had philosophers scratching their heads from Descartes's time until today. Numerous solutions have been offered, but still the debate rages on. The difficulty of accounting for the interaction between mind and body has led many contemporary philosophers to reject dualism altogether, and to view the mind as a physical thing. Those who reject the existence of a separate mind-substance are known as *physicalists*.

One of the fiercest critics of dualism was the Oxford philosopher Gilbert Ryle (1900–76). It was he who coined the phrase 'the ghost in the machine' to lampoon the dualist view of mind and body. The point being, of course, how does the ghost move the machine?

19. HOW DID THAT HAPPEN?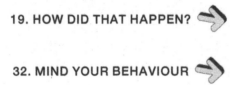

32. MIND YOUR BEHAVIOUR

19

HOW DID THAT HAPPEN?

According to Descartes, the mind and body are separate things. Each of us has an immaterial mind and a material body. But, as we saw in the previous chapter, this raises the thorny question of how two such very different substances can possibly interact. How can mental processes cause bodily movements? And how can bodily processes give rise to thoughts, feelings and perceptions?

Occasionalism

Over the years, various solutions to the mind-body problem have been proposed. An interesting albeit bizarre one was proposed by Nicolas Malebranche (1638–1715), an ardent admirer of Descartes, and a fellow Frenchman.

Rather than suggesting some kind of mechanism by which mind and body might conceivably interact, Malebranche denied that they interact at all. He claimed that mental events do not cause physical events and that physical events do not cause mental events. This flies somewhat in the face of the evidence. After all, can anyone doubt that by an act of thought I can cause my finger to move? Or that cutting my finger will cause me pain?

Malebranche's response is that, contrary to appearances, my thoughts do not cause my finger to move; and the cutting of my flesh does not cause me pain. It is God, and God alone, who moves my finger; and it is God, and God alone, who causes my pain. My intention to move my finger is merely the *occasion* that prompts God to move the finger for me; and the cutting of my flesh is merely the *occasion* that prompts God to cause me pain.

Malebranche's theory, which goes by the name *occasionalism*, holds that there is only one true cause, namely God. It neatly disposes of the problem of mind-body interaction by denying that there *is* any interaction. But occasionalism isn't just an *ad hoc* response to the mind-body problem. Malebranche advances a number of positive arguments in support of it.

Necessary connection

'A true cause', wrote Malebranche, '. . . is one such that the mind perceives a necessary connection between it and its effect.' In other words, we can only claim that A causes B if we can see that A *necessarily* leads to B.

But we cannot perceive any necessary connections between mental states and bodily states. For example, I might form the intention to move my finger and yet my finger might remain unmoved; my flesh might be cut and yet I might feel no pain. Similarly we can perceive no necessary connections between physical states and other physical states. When one billiard ball strikes another we expect the first ball to impart motion to the second. But this is only because we have plenty of experience of similar collisions, not because the one event *necessarily* implies the other. Experience aside, it is perfectly conceivable that the second ball might remain stationary . . . or disappear . . . or allow the first ball to pass right through itself.

In short, we never perceive necessary connections between mind-body events, body-mind events or even body-body events. Therefore no true causes operate between them.

In the case of God, though, things are different. God's omnipotence guarantees that whatever He wills to occur will occur. If God wills my finger to move, it will, of necessity, move. If He wills me to feel pain, I will, of necessity, feel pain. Malebranche wrote: 'Now the mind perceives a necessary connection only between the will of an infinitely perfect being and its effects. Therefore, it is only God who is the true cause and who truly has the power to move bodies.'

Of course, Malebranche's initial premise, that a true cause is one such that we perceive a necessary connection between it and its effect, is not uncontentious. It is one thing to insist upon a necessary connection between a cause and its effect but quite another thing to insist that the mind is able to perceive that connection.

Continuous creation

Another of Malebranche's arguments draws upon a principle found in Descartes's *Meditations*, namely that God conserves the world by continuously creating it. Descartes claimed that just because something existed a little while ago it doesn't follow that it must exist now. There must, he said, be some cause that keeps it in existence. This cause is God, who keeps it in existence by creating it afresh each moment.

Descartes didn't really justify this doctrine. He merely stated that 'it is clear to anyone who attentively considers the nature of time' and assured us that it is 'something which all metaphysicians affirm as a manifest truth'.

From the doctrine of continuous creation, Malebranche deduced that God may conserve a body either by continuously creating it in the same place, in which case it is stationary; or by continuously creating it in different places, in which case it is in motion. But this means that one body can never act upon another body so as to move it. Nor can a mind act upon a body so as to move it. Whether a body is in motion or at rest depends entirely upon the location at which God chooses to recreate it moment by moment:

> For what is more evident than that if God, for example, keeps a body always in one place, then no creature could move it to another? Or that no man could even move his own arm unless God wills to concur in doing that which ungrateful stupid man thinks he is doing by himself?

Once again, we might feel inclined to doubt Malebranche's premise here: namely that God conserves the world by continuous creation. Interestingly though, most of his contemporaries, even his most vociferous opponents, were willing to grant it.

Bizarre but influential

Despite being an implausible theory, Malebranche's occasionalism has provided food for thought for some first-rate philosophers. Leibniz and Berkeley, though not convinced, were certainly influenced by it.

Even the arch-sceptic David Hume, who dismissed occasionalism as a 'fairy land' theory, was strongly influenced by Malebranche's claim that necessary connection is central to the notion of cause and effect. Hume claimed that, since neither the mind nor the senses can ever discover any necessary connection between any two objects or events, we can have no solid reasons for attributing causal powers to either minds or bodies. Hume even denied that we can discover a necessary connection between the Divine will and any event.

 18. THE GHOST IN THE MACHINE

20. LEIBNIZ'S FANTASTIC FAIRYTALE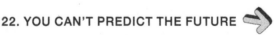

22. YOU CAN'T PREDICT THE FUTURE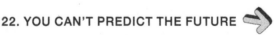

20

LEIBNIZ'S FANTASTIC FAIRYTALE

Of all the weird ideas in philosophy, Leibniz's *Monadology* is right up there with the weirdest. So incredibly and mind-bogglingly weird, in fact, that it provided the inspiration for this entire book.

The English philosopher Bertrand Russell reported that after reading up on Leibniz for a series of lectures he 'felt – as many others have felt – that the *Monadology* was a kind of fantastic fairy tale, coherent perhaps, but wholly arbitrary'. He went on to say, in fairness, that further research revealed much of interest and value in Leibniz's ideas.

Monads

The *Monadology*, written in 1714, is a concise summary of the German philosopher Gottfried Leibniz's ideas about simple substances: the most basic constituents of reality.

As we have seen, Descartes had previously claimed that the world contains two kinds of substance: *matter* which is characterised by extension; and *mind* which is characterised by thought. Leibniz rejected this dualist view, claiming that reality is purely mental.

Empirical objects (the objects we perceive with our senses) are, Leibniz said, divisible. They are aggregates or compounds. They must, therefore, be composed of simple substances 'for the compound is only a collection or *aggregatum* of simple substances'. These simple substances cannot be extended – they can have neither size nor shape – since then they could be divided still further and would not be simple after all.

Simple substances, being unextended, must be immaterial. This means that they must be minds, albeit perhaps of a very rudimentary sort. The fundamental units of nature are, therefore, immaterial soul-like entities which Leibniz labelled *monads*.

Monadology

What else can be said about monads? Well, after much metaphysical musing Leibniz deduced the following monadic properties.

There are infinite numbers of monads, all of them different. Since they are simple, nothing can be added to them or subtracted from them. This means that they can neither grow nor decay. God can create or annihilate them but otherwise they cannot come into or go out of being.

Monads are, in Leibniz's terminology, 'windowless'. This means that they have no means of communicating or interacting with the rest of the world. No monad affects or is affected by any other. Even so, each monad is constantly changing and developing. But its changes are internally driven.

Monads are, to use a modern term, pre-programmed. Each changing state of a monad is the outworking of an inner drive, pre-programmed by God at creation. Furthermore, since monads are immaterial, these changes must be changes of mental rather than physical state.

Although monads do not interact or communicate with one another, each one is, in Leibniz's words, 'a perpetual living mirror of the universe'. What this means is that each monad has a 'perception', an inner representation, of everything else that exists. This inner representation changes to reflect changes in the environment. Not because the environment affects the monad (monads are windowless), but because God has pre-programmed it that way.

The weird and wonderful world of monads

The world, then, is made up of simple, immaterial, soul-like entities called monads. An inanimate object such as a rock is an aggregate of infinitely many 'bare' monads. These bare monads have perceptions only in a very rudimentary sense. That is, their inner representation of the universe is unclear and indistinct.

Higher up the scale, an animal is an aggregate of monads united by a single dominant monad, a 'soul', which has not only perception but also conscious awareness. Further still up the scale, a human being is an aggregate of monads whose dominant monad possesses not only conscious awareness but also reason. This monad earns the title 'mind'.

Pre-established harmony

Monads are windowless. They do not interact with one another. How then do we explain the apparent interaction we observe between the objects of experience? And how do we account for the fact that each monad mirrors, or perceives, the universe?

Leibniz accounted for all of this by appealing to the notion of 'pre-established harmony'. God, he said, has made each monad such that its internally-driven changes are precisely synchronised with those of all other monads. It is as though a clockmaker has made a number of clocks that all chime at the same instant. They synchronise not because they exert any influence upon one another but because they are constructed with such accuracy. In a similar way, God has created an infinite number of perfectly synchronised monads.

So, for example, when I kick a stone it skids across the ground not because I influence it in any way, but because my monads and the stone's monads have been programmed since creation to behave in precisely that way at that precise moment.

Space and time are unreal

Sharp-minded readers may be wondering how it is that non-extended monads can combine together to form the extended objects we perceive around us. It seems pretty clear that no matter how many non-sized objects you combine, even an infinite number, you'll never manage to produce an object of any size.

Leibniz answer is that there *are* no extended objects. The objects of the senses *appear* to have shapes and sizes. Space *appears* to be real. But this is just how things seem. In reality, bodies are no more extended than the monads that constitute them. The world is not itself extended, but it is *represented* to us as extended.

Your dominant monad, your mind, sees the world from a certain perspective. My dominant monad, my mind, sees the world from a different perspective. The illusion of space helps us to make sense of the world, each from our own perspective. But space itself is unreal. (Think of those computer games where players explore and interact with a virtual world. Objects in that world appear to be located in three-dimensional space. But they're not really. That's just the way they're represented to us.)

Similar considerations apply to time, which is also, according to Leibniz, unreal.

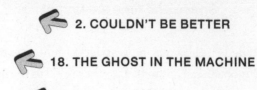

21

OUCH! I FEEL GOOD

The Greek philosopher Epicurus (341–270 BC) said that a wise man can be happy even on the rack. This sounds absurd. Indeed, Aristotle rejected the idea as 'nonsense', arguing that since pleasure is an essential ingredient of happiness the happy man must be reliant to some extent upon circumstances.

According to one old story, an earnest undergraduate once asked Benjamin Jowett, the Oxford classicist and theologian, if he thought a good man really could be happy on the rack. Dr Jowett considered the matter carefully and then replied, 'Perhaps a very good man – on a very bad rack!'

The trials and tribulations of Epicurus

The criticisms of Aristotle and Dr Jowett notwithstanding, Epicurus himself demonstrated a remarkable ability to endure discomfort cheerfully. He suffered all his life from ill health and died a very painful death. But he bore his sufferings with exemplary fortitude and good humour. On the day he died, he wrote a charming and cheerful note to a friend:

> On this truly happy day of my life, as I am at the point of death, I write this to you. The diseases in my bladder and stomach are pursuing their usual course . . . but against all this is the joy in my heart at the recollection of my conversations with you.

In Shakespeare's *Much Ado About Nothing*, the ageing nobleman Leonato quips: 'There was never yet philosopher that could endure the toothache patiently.' Clearly he was unacquainted with Epicurus. Even so, Epicurus' claim that a wise man can be happy even under torture remains puzzling. Not least because it appears to go against a fundamental precept of his own philosophy, namely that pleasure is the only good.

Pleasure and pain

'Pleasure is the beginning and end of the blessed life', claimed Epicurus. In other words, it is in pleasure and in pleasure alone that happiness consists. The aim of life is to be happy; and in practical terms this means maximising pleasure and minimising pain.

This is not to say that Epicurus endorsed the headlong pursuit of pleasure. He recognised that some pleasures (overeating, for example) lead to pain and therefore ought to be avoided. In fact, he held that the avoidance of pain plays a more important role than the pursuit of pleasure in our quest for happiness. His advice, therefore, was to cultivate simple and lasting pleasures which have few ill effects.

Good wholesome food, the company of friends and a simple stress-free way of life was Epicurus' prescription for a happy life. Accordingly, he and his disciples formed a self-sufficient community in a garden just outside Athens where they lived simply and happily together. Their no-frills, back-to-basics lifestyle was designed to secure health of the body and tranquility of the soul.

Avoid pain – on the rack?

All of this prompts an obvious and important question. How can someone who places so much emphasis on the avoidance of pain claim that a wise man can be happy on the rack? The whole point of the rack is, after all, to inflict pain. Surely, by Epicurus' account, nobody could be more *miserable* than a torture victim.

Two points ought to be made here. First of all, when Epicurus said that happiness consists in pleasure alone he did not mean the mere pleasure of the moment, but rather pleasure over the course of a lifetime. This is clear from his eschewing of short-term pleasures in favour of lasting ones.

Second, Epicurus held that intellectual pleasures are superior to physical ones, and that physical pains are less grievous than mental ones. Intellectual pleasures are valued above physical ones not because they are intrinsically better, but because they lie more directly under our control (we can direct our thoughts even when we cannot direct our circumstances). Physical pains are less grievous than mental ones because severe bodily pains tend to be short-lived, and once they are over they are over. Mental anguish, on the other hand, extends to the recollection of past evils and the dread of future ones. '[T]he flesh endures the storms of the present alone', wrote Epicurus, 'the mind those of the past and future as well . . . '

Non-severe pains, even when prolonged, need not prevent the wise man from being happy. He can follow Epicurus' example and focus his mind on happy thoughts. But what about the victim on the rack?

Well, clearly he must suffer and 'give vent to cries and moans'. But he will have the consolation of knowing that his agonies are likely to be short-lived, and that his life, viewed as a whole, may still be considered a happy one. Furthermore, even amidst his torments, he can think positive thoughts and feel 'gratitude towards friends, present and absent alike'.

A grain of truth

Ultimately, the claim that the wise man will be happy on the rack is unconvincing. Under sufficient torture it is doubtful that even the most disciplined mind could focus on much else beside the present pain. Nonetheless, there remains a grain of truth in what Epicurus said. The circumstances of his own life suggest that it is possible to live fully and happily in spite of physical suffering.

1. NOT *BAD*. JUST MISGUIDED

12. DAN BROWN VS. SHAKESPEARE

23. AN END TO SUFFERING

22

YOU CAN'T PREDICT THE FUTURE

If I lift my pencil a few inches above the table and then let go, what will happen? Clearly, it will fall back down. Everyone knows *that*. But how do we know? What makes us so certain?

If pressed for an answer, most people would probably reply that pencils have always behaved that way; that we know pencils will fall in the future because they have always fallen in the past.

If pressed further, as to *why* we believe pencils will continue to fall as previously, we might appeal to the law of gravity. Objects such as pencils, we will say, always fall under the influence of gravity unless prevented from doing so. But this raises the question of how we know that the law of gravity will continue to operate in the future as it has done in the past; and we end up back where we started.

Ultimately, then, our belief that unsupported pencils will

fall relies on the assumption that the future will resemble the past. It's a natural assumption. It's one that we all make, and, indeed, one that we cannot help but make (try dropping a pencil and keeping an open mind about what will happen). But can we justify it? Do we have any valid reason for believing that because pencils have fallen in the past they will continue to do so in the future?

Deduction and induction

Consider the following argument.

> 1. In the past, every pencil that was ever dropped fell to the ground.
>
> 2. This pencil is about to be dropped. *Therefore*
>
> 3. It will fall to the ground.

The first thing to notice is that this isn't what philosophers call a deductively valid argument.

A deductively valid argument is one in which the premises lead inescapably, via cast-iron logic, to the conclusion. For example:

> 1. All men are mortal.
>
> 2. Socrates is a man. *Therefore*
>
> 3. Socrates is mortal.

Anyone can see that if the premises of this argument are true (if all men are indeed mortal; and if Socrates is indeed a man) then it follows logically that the conclusion *must* be true also.

But this is not the case for the dropped pencil argument. There, the premises do not guarantee the conclusion. There is no *logical* reason why the next pencil shouldn't behave differently from all of the previous ones. We may not expect it to do so, but it's perfectly conceivable that it might. So the argument is not deductively valid.

Nonetheless, it has to be admitted that the dropped pencil argument seems compelling. It is, in fact, a different type of argument, namely an *inductive* one. An inductive argument is one in which a general conclusion is drawn from a specific number of instances. For example, after observing a large number of swans, and noting that they are all white, inductive reasoning might lead us to conclude that all swans are white.

We use inductive reasoning all the time. It is essential to our survival. Without it we would have no reason to expect fire to burn us, food to nourish us or day to follow night. Our experience of the world would be chaotic and unpredictable.

The problem of induction

But induction, however essential, is not without its difficulties. In the first place, it is not one hundred per cent reliable. Inductive arguments never quite guarantee their conclusions. Prior to 1697, Europeans had observed millions of swans, all of them white. Inductive reasoning led them to conclude that all swans are white. But the discovery of the Australian black swan demonstrated this conclusion to be false.

Secondly, there's the more basic question of whether we can justify our use of induction at all. Inductive reasoning relies on the assumption that what has happened in the past serves as a reliable guide to what will happen in the future. But what justifies this assumption? This question, now labelled the *problem of induction*, was posed by the great Scottish philosopher David Hume (1711–76) and has been a thorn in philosophy's side ever since.

But hasn't induction always worked so far?

So what *does* justify us in thinking that because dropped pencils have always fallen in the past they will continue to do so in the future; or that because the sun has risen every morning previously it will do so again tomorrow? More generally, what reason do we have for believing that the laws of nature will continue to operate tomorrow as they have in the past?

The obvious reply is that we are justified in believing the future will resemble the past because this assumption has always proved reliable thus far. Every waking minute of every single day we rely on induction for our very survival. Furthermore, all our scientific and technological advances have relied on the assumption that there are predictable regularities in the natural world.

But this defence itself relies on induction. As Bertrand

Russell pointed out in *The Problems of Philosophy*: 'such an argument really begs the very question at issue. We have experience of past futures, but not of future futures, and the question is: Will future futures resemble past futures?'

If we try to justify our belief that the future will resemble the past by pointing out that it has always done so previously, we are guilty of circular reasoning: assuming the very thing we're supposed to be proving.

The problem of induction is one of philosophy's most intractable problems. We cannot help but believe in the continued uniformity of nature, and this belief has served us well in the past. Even so, we cannot prove deductively that nature is uniform; and our experience teaches us only that nature has been uniform up to now. We use the principle of induction constantly in our reasoning, but seem unable to reason our way *to* it.

But perhaps the problem of induction is a pseudo-problem. Some philosophers claim that the entire attempt to justify induction is misguided; that we cannot rationally justify induction because induction is part of what it *means* to be rational. If so, then it makes no more sense to ask 'Is induction rational?' than it does to ask 'Is the law legal?'

19. HOW DID THAT HAPPEN?

42. SCIENTIFICALLY UNPROVEN

23

AN END TO SUFFERING

'Both in the past and now, I set forth only this: suffering and the end of suffering', said the Buddha. His message from first to last was about suffering: how it arises and how it can be overcome.

There have been plenty of thinkers who have addressed themselves to the same problem. But few, if any, with such single-mindedness. The Buddha's ideas about the origin and pervasiveness of suffering are original and profound. His ideas about how it can be overcome are, quite simply, startling.

Life is suffering

The cornerstone of the Buddha's philosophy, his First Noble Truth, is that *life is suffering*. He made this point emphatically: 'Birth is suffering, old age is suffering, sickness is suffering, death is suffering. Involvement with what is unpleasant is suffering. Separation from what is pleasant is suffering. Also, not getting what one wants and strives for is suffering.'

Suffering isn't something that sometimes attaches itself to one's life; something that can be avoided with a bit of good luck and careful management. Suffering is woven into the very fabric of life. Life *is* suffering.

The cause of suffering

Buddha's next insight, his Second Noble Truth, is that *suffering is caused by craving*.

The world, Buddha tells us, is impermanent. It, and everything in it, is in constant flux. Nothing remains the same from one moment to the next. As part of the world, we too are impermanent. Our bodies are visibly changing organisms, subject to decay and destined to perish. And our minds are even less stable than our bodies. Impressions, ideas, sensations and desires arise within us and replace one another every moment, so that the mind is constantly 'perishing as one thing and springing up as another'.

This impermanence in the physical and mental world leads to suffering. It is part of our nature to crave stable and lasting happiness. But, due to the impermanence of things, any happiness we achieve can only be fleeting and unsatisfactory.

Our craving fuels the fire of suffering. It makes us cling to possessions, to persons, to pleasant experiences and to life itself. But all of these things are impermanent and unsatisfactory. And so we attach ourselves to new objects, which in turn fail to satisfy. And so it goes. And so it goes.

Not even death releases us from suffering. The same craving that fuels the fires of suffering in this life propels us into the next. As we saw in chapter 10, actions motivated by desire produce karma which drives samsara, the cycle of death and rebirth (the concepts of karma and samsara are fundamental to Buddhism as well as Hinduism). So we are born and reborn into lives of suffering.

The end of suffering

All of this makes suffering seem inevitable and inescapable. Yet the Buddha assures us that *suffering can have an end*. This is the Third Noble Truth.

Suffering ceases when we root out its cause: when we cease craving. Buddha said, 'This, O Monks, is the Truth of the Cessation of Suffering. It is the utter cessation of that craving, the withdrawal from it, the renouncing of it, the rejection of it, liberation from it, non-attachment.'

Craving fuels the fire of suffering. So to bring an end to suffering we must cease from craving. This is the Buddha's radical, but very logical, solution to the problem of suffering.

Once craving ceases, *nirvana*, or enlightenment, is attained. This is a state of total peace and freedom; a state of deep spiritual joy; a state of inner purity and stability. The enlightened individual grasps after nothing and is freed from anxiety and dissatisfaction; from suffering.

After death, the enlightened person is not reborn. So what happens to him? This is a mystery. The Buddha refused to speak about the nature of 'final nirvana', perhaps because conceptual language is not up to the task of describing it. And in any case, such metaphysical speculations only distract us from the more important task of actually attaining enlightenment.

Mostly, then, Buddhists describe the state of final nirvana in negative terms such as 'absence of desire'. That said, it is regarded, in some vague sense, as being a state of supreme blessedness.

The pathway

To bring an end to suffering, then, we must cease from craving. But how is this to be achieved? Is it even possible? Buddha's answer, his Fourth Noble Truth, is that *there is a path which leads to the end of suffering.*

The way to end suffering and achieve nirvana is, Buddha said, to follow the Eightfold Path. This is a way of life designed to develop virtue and knowledge. It consists of eight factors: right understanding, right thought, right speech, right action, right livelihood, right effort, right mindfulness and right concentration. The Eightfold Path is a path of intellectual, emotional and moral self-transformation. It is the means through which ignorance and selfish desire can be overcome and nirvana attained.

Philosophy or religion?

Is Buddhism a philosophy or a religion? Well, there's a lot of debate about that. But there is no doubt that the Buddha's views are of great philosophical interest whether or not we buy into samsara, nirvana and all that stuff.

At the core of the Buddha's philosophy is the notion that suffering and dissatisfaction originate in the way the mind reacts to the circumstances of life. Nothing in this world is permanent: success gives way to failure; pleasure gives way to pain; life gives way to death. Ultimately, none of this is under our control. But what we *can* control, or can at least learn to control, is the way our mind reacts to those things.

This is an interesting and profound insight. The Greek philosopher Epicurus made a similar point, as we saw in chapter 21, when he said that we can direct our thoughts even when we cannot direct our circumstances, and can therefore live contentedly despite life's ups and downs.

 10. COSMIC COMEUPPANCE

21. OUCH! I FEEL GOOD

26. ONE HAND CLAPPING

24

THE WEAKER SEX?

The great philosophers have had plenty to say about women. Much of it derogatory.

Plato and Aristotle on women

Towards the end of the *Timaeus*, Plato, discoursing on the formation of the universe, offered the following gem: 'On the subject of animals, then, the following remarks may be offered. Of the men who came into the world, those who were cowards or led unrighteous lives may with reason be supposed to have changed into the nature of women in the second generation.'

In fairness, it must be said that Plato sometimes advanced more egalitarian views. In the *Republic* he advocated equal training and opportunities for men and women, and asserted that natural capacities are similarly distributed in each sex. Though even there he added the (somewhat puzzling, given the context) caveat: 'though in all women will be the weaker partners'.

Aristotle too held that women are inferior to men, and said so quite explicitly: 'And it is clear that the rule of the soul over the body, and of the mind and the rational element over the passionate, is natural and expedient . . . [T]he male is by nature superior, and the female inferior; and the one rules, and the other is ruled; this principle, of necessity, extends to all mankind.'

Schopenhauer, *On Women*

The view that men are 'rational' while women are 'passionate', and that women are therefore inferior, crops up not infrequently in the philosophical canon. But nowhere is it expressed more forcibly, and with as little ceremony, as in the German philosopher Arthur Schopenhauer's notorious essay, *On Women*.

The tenor of Schopenhauer's essay is set right at the beginning with a quotation from the French writer Jouy: 'Without women the beginning of our life would be helpless; the middle, devoid of pleasure; and the end, of consolation.' This, Schopenhauer thought, accurately represents the role and value of women.

He went on to say that women are less rational than men; prefer trifling matters to important ones; lack a sense of justice; are instinctively crafty; are incorrigible liars; are incapable of appreciating, let alone creating, great art; and so on; and so on.

He bemoaned the fact that wives squander their husbands' hard-earned cash, and that widows fritter away the fortunes their husbands leave behind. 'In their hearts, women imagine that men are born to earn money', he wrote. Towards the end of the essay he advocated polygamy, arguing that this would be to women's benefit since 'among the polygamous races every woman is provided for'.

Many of Schopenhauer's views were, it must be said, pretty commonplace at the time. But no other major philosopher has, to my knowledge, expressed them in such bluntly disparaging terms. Here are a few quotations, picked almost at random:

> 'The sight of the female form tells us that woman is not destined for great work, either intellectual or physical. She bears the guilt of life not by doing but by suffering . . .'

> 'It therefore lies in the nature of women to regard everything merely as a means to win the man; and their interest in anything else is always only simulated . . . it ends in coquetry and aping.'

> 'Only the male intellect, clouded by the sexual impulse, could call the undersized, narrow-shouldered, broadhipped, and short-legged sex the fair sex; for in this impulse is to be found its whole beauty.'

> 'Women are qualified to be the nurses and governesses of our earliest childhood by the very fact that they are themselves childish, trifling, and short-sighted, in a word, are all their lives grown-up children . . .'

The 'credit side'

In his excellent book, *The Philosophy of Schopenhauer*, the broadcaster and writer Bryan Magee says that the essay *On Women*, though intolerant and one-sided, is not the unremitting tirade against women that some people imagine it to be since 'it includes a balance sheet with a credit as well as a debit side'. But perhaps Magee is being a little forbearing. Most of the compliments Schopenhauer paid to women in the essay are, in fact, blatantly back-handed.

Schopenhauer did, to be sure, say that women reach maturity in reasoning earlier in their development than men do. But only after remarking that 'the nobler and more perfect a thing is, the later and more slowly does it come to maturity.' He did, undeniably, grant that women can see easily through dissimulation in others. But only because dissimulation is 'inborn' in them, and they themselves make use of it 'on every occasion'. He did, most certainly, credit women with showing more sympathy for the unfortunate than men. But only 'in consequence of their weak faculty of reason'. His praise is scarcely less disparaging than his censure.

The 'argument'

There has been little sustained criticism of the arguments Schopenhauer presented in *On Women*. The reason for this, I think, is that there really isn't very much argument *to* criticise. The essay is really just a rant.

As far as I can decipher it, his argument, such as it is, runs as follows. Women are weak, unreasoning, dishonest, childish, untalented, etc. This shows that they are inferior to men. Therefore they ought to be kept in their place.

Ultimately, then, his argument is built upon a set of sweeping and outrageously inaccurate generalisations. Either Schopenhauer had a very jaundiced view of women or he was acquainted with a very unrepresentative sample of them.

The essay's appeal

In his introduction to the *Cambridge Companion to Schopenhauer*, Christopher Janaway describes *On Women* as 'a nasty, gratuitous piece of misogyny, whose only conceivable merit is that it is written with his characteristic vigour'.

When it was first published the essay became very popular. It still attracts a lot of casual, though not scholarly, interest today. But there can be little doubt that it is Schopenhauer's vigour of expression rather than the quality of his argument that has made it so widely known.

 **3. COULDN'T BE WORSE**

25

SELFISHNESS IS A VIRTUE

Most of us consider altruistic acts to be good and praiseworthy, and consider self-interested acts to be morally neutral, at best. We admire the talented doctor who puts her career on hold to treat malaria victims in Uganda. We do not so admire the brilliant surgeon who rakes in the cash doing plastic surgery in Tinseltown.

Altruism is, on the whole, a good thing; selfishness is, on the whole, not such a good thing. Few would argue with that. But the Russian-American novelist and philosopher Ayn Rand (1905–82) saw things differently. She claimed that selfishness is a virtue and altruism an 'evil'.

Egoism vs. altruism

Rand was an *egoist*. Not in the sense of having an exaggerated sense of her own importance (though that may, perhaps, have been true) but in the sense of subscribing to the philosophical doctrine of ethical egoism. This holds that our actions ought always to be grounded in self-interest; that selfishness is morally right and good.

How did Rand reach this conclusion? Well, she began by stressing the intrinsic worth of each individual human being. Each person, she argued, by reason of their intrinsic worth has the right to pursue their own happiness and well-being. Egoism recognises this. Altruism, on the other hand, denies individual worth. It holds that man has no right to exist for himself but must justify his existence through serving others. It upholds 'the *self* as the standard of evil, the *selfless* as a standard of the good'. It demands self-sacrifice, self-denial and self-destruction.

Traditionally we have been led to believe that selfishness is wrong, said Rand. The image of the selfish man has been that of an unfeeling brute trampling others underfoot in pursuit of his own mindless whims. We have been asked to choose between egoism, characterised as the sacrifice of others to the self, and altruism, characterised as the sacrifice of the self to others. This has been presented as a stark choice between evil and good; and so we have had little alternative but to choose altruism.

Rand, however, pointed out that 'selfishness' simply means pursuing one's own ends and interests, and ought not to be understood with the usual negative connotations of brutishness and disdain for others. Similarly, egoism consists merely in the pursuit of one's own happiness and well-being. It does not

– indeed ought not to – require the sacrifice of others to the self.

This conception of egoism is neatly summed up by John Galt, a character in Ayn Rand's philosophical novel *Atlas Shrugged*: 'I swear – by my life and my love of it – that I will never live for the sake of another man, nor ask another man to live for mine.'

The evils of altruism

By Rand's account, then, altruism denies the intrinsic worth of the individual. She argued, further, that altruism has evil consequences.

How so? Well, altruism teaches man that morality is his enemy. He grudgingly sacrifices himself for others and hopes that they may occasionally do the same for him. But this leads to bitterness and resentment all round. 'Do not confuse altruism with kindness, good will or respect for the rights of others', Rand warned. Altruism makes such virtues impossible. Egoism, on the other hand, makes all of the principal virtues possible.

The virtue of selfishness

Although Rand advocated the pursuit of self-interest, she repudiated what she called 'whim-worship' or 'hedonism'. Man, she claimed, is fundamentally a rational creature. Reason is his basic tool of survival. To be fully human, therefore, he must pursue his own *rational* self-interest. Anyone driven by mere whims, emotions or instinct is guilty of living on a sub-human level.

The rational egoist lives life by three fundamental principles: reason, purpose and self-esteem. These support virtues such as honesty, justice, integrity, independence and the like. But they do not require the sacrifice of anyone to anyone else. Rand wrote: 'Do not hide behind such superficialities as whether you should or should not give a dime to a beggar. That is not the issue. The issue is whether you do or do not have the right to exist without giving him that dime.'

When men each pursue their own rational self-interest, Rand argued, those interests will not clash. Conflicts arise only when men desire the unearned; when they require the sacrifice of others to themselves. Reason dictates that men deal with one another through persuasion and cooperation rather than through threats, force or fraud.

Is Rand right?

Stirring stuff! Here, at last, we have an ethics that doesn't oblige us to comfort the afflicted, tend the sick or feed the hungry! But does Rand's argument stand up to scrutiny? Is it really OK – nay, virtuous – to be selfish?

A common objection to Rand's line of reasoning is that she presents us with a false dichotomy. That is, she presents us with two alternatives as though they were mutually exclusive when, in fact, they're not. She says, in effect, that you can be an out-and-out altruist and act only for others, or you can be an out-and-out egoist and act only for yourself.

But what's to stop you from taking the middle ground? What's to prevent you from sometimes acting for yourself and sometimes acting for others? You may even decide that since you are generally best placed to attend to your own needs while other people are generally best placed to attend to theirs, you ought, in the main, to act for yourself. But, recognising the intrinsic worth of individuals other than yourself, you may still sometimes feel an obligation to help others, especially those who are powerless to act for themselves.

Rand accuses previous moral thinkers of presenting us with a stark choice between altruism and egoism. But this accusation is unjust. Most of them grant that our own interests are of at least equal value with the interests of others. Is it not, then, Rand herself who polarises the choice?

Rand's influence

Ayn Rand's work hasn't had much influence on mainstream academic philosophy, but it has attracted a huge popular following. A survey conducted by the US Library of Congress and the Book of the Month Club once asked readers which book had most influenced their lives. *Atlas Shrugged* came second only to the Bible.

Her work is loathed, however, quite as often as it is admired. Her detractors often claim that her novels appeal mainly to the immature. A well-known quotation from writer John Rogers, circulated on the Internet, expresses this point of view beautifully. 'There are two novels that can change a book-ish fourteen-year-old's life: *The Lord of the Rings* and *Atlas Shrugged*. One is a childish fantasy that often engenders a life-long obsession with its unbelievable heroes, leading to an emotionally stunted, socially crippled adulthood, unable to deal with the real world. The other, of course, involves orcs.'

 4. SELFISH MOTIVES

31. DUTY CALLS! ➡

40. RULES . . . RULES . . . RULES ➡

26

ONE HAND CLAPPING

What is the sound of one hand clapping? Does a dog have a Buddha Nature? Does the wind move the flag, or does the flag move the wind? Your inability to answer – or even to understand – these questions may help you to achieve enlightenment.

Welcome to the strange world of Zen: a philosophy which says that the key to enlightenment is to stop thinking. That's right: *stop* thinking.

Ultimate reality

Many Western philosophers have sought to understand the ultimate nature of reality. Some of their ideas on the subject, such as Plato's theory of Forms, Leibniz's monadology and Berkley's idealism, have been discussed in previous chapters.

Eastern philosophers seek a similar understanding. They too want to know how things ultimately are. But their approach is different. Unlike their Western counterparts, they tend to view meditation, intuition and mystical experience as valid means of acquiring knowledge. They don't rely solely on critical analysis and logical reasoning.

For both the Eastern sage and the Western philosopher, the quest for understanding usually proves long and difficult. Western philosophers may spend decades thinking through and refining their systems. Eastern sages may spend a lifetime – or many lifetimes – in their search for enlightenment. But the Japanese philosopher Eisai (1141–1215), the founder of Zen, taught that this need not be the case; that enlightenment can happen in a flash.

Zen and the art of enlightenment

Zen is a distinctive form of Buddhism which originated in China, as *Ch'an* Buddhism, during the sixth century, and later spread to Japan. The Japanese word *Zen* is derived from the Chinese *Ch'an* which is, in turn, derived from the Sanskrit *dhyana*, meaning 'meditation'. The especially strong emphasis on meditation is what distinguishes Zen from other forms of Buddhism. It was, in fact, Eisai who introduced meditation to Japan.

The ultimate aim of Zen is to achieve enlightenment: a state in which all distinctions, such as that between the knower and the known and the self and the non-self, disappear. This definition is necessarily vague and unsatisfactory, however, because the true nature of enlightenment cannot be expressed in words. It can be understood only by those who have experienced it.

In fact, words and concepts stand in the way of enlightenment. According to Zen, reality cannot be grasped by ordinary ways of thinking. It can be understood only at an intuitive, non-conceptual level. So it is important not to get too hung up on thinking; not to get tangled in the 'net of words'.

The point of Zen meditation is, therefore, not to think but to step outside the limits of thought; to 'make the calculating mind die'. If this all sounds paradoxical and obscure, that's only to be expected. Zen *is* paradoxical and obscure. It cannot be conceptualised. Any attempt to express the inexpressible must end up in paradox.

Everyday Zen

Despite Zen's strong emphasis on meditation, Zen practitioners do not withdraw from everyday life. Far from it. An important aspect of spiritual development in Zen is to go about one's everyday tasks simply, naturally and without effort; acting intuitively rather than constantly evaluating one's actions.

In Zen, everyday activities such as gardening and drinking tea can thus become forms of meditation. As can art forms such as painting, calligraphy and flower-arranging, and disciplines such as archery. (Eisai introduced tea to Japan from China: partly to help his monks to stay awake, but mostly so that they could use the act of preparing and serving it as an opportunity to practise meditation.)

At first, it takes enormous effort to act effortlessly, and great purpose of mind to act without purpose. But eventually it comes naturally. The resulting freedom from attachments and desires makes for a more harmonious and peaceful existence, and paves the way for enlightenment.

Aids to enlightenment

There are two main schools of Zen. One of them, the Soto School, holds that enlightenment is attained gradually through years of discipline. The other, the Rinzai School, which was founded by Eisai, holds that enlightenment can be achieved at any time, instantaneously.

In the Rinzai School, Zen masters make use of *koans* to help students in their quest for enlightenment. Koans are baffling statements, questions, riddles or dialogues. The most famous koan is the question, 'What is the sound of one hand clapping?' The idea is to force the mind out of its ordinary ways of thinking, and open it up to the non-conceptual level of understanding required to grasp reality.

Sometimes, koans take the form of question-and-answer sessions between master and pupil. In one celebrated exchange, a pupil asked, 'What is the first principle of

Buddhism?' The master replied, 'If I told you, it would be the second principle!'

Alternatively, a student's question about some aspect of Buddhism may be answered by an apparent non sequitur: perhaps a statement about the weather or the price of beans. One monk asked, 'Why did the Bodhidharma [a Zen patriarch] come to China?' His master replied, 'The cypress tree in the courtyard.'

When a pupil is on the verge of enlightenment, the master may resort to even more unconventional methods such as yelling or hitting. One master went so far as to cut off a student's finger. Timed correctly, these actions may – it is said – provide the final psychological push needed to trigger enlightenment.

Ineffable wisdom?

Zen claims to be beyond reason; beyond rationality; beyond logic; beyond conceptualisation; beyond expression.

But, in that case, how are we, the unenlightened, to evaluate it? And how are we to assess the claims of its devotees? If someone tells us that his intuition has revealed to him truths that cannot be expressed, he may, for all we know, be correct. But, on the other hand, he may be mistaken, misguided – or even deliberately misleading us.

One Zen monk asked, 'What is Buddha?' His master replied, 'Three pounds of flax.' Perhaps this is inscrutable wisdom. Then again, perhaps not.

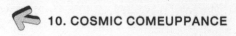 **10. COSMIC COMEUPPANCE**

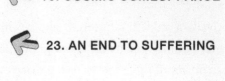 **23. AN END TO SUFFERING**

40. RULES . . . RULES . . . RULES

27

THOU SHALT KILL

Whatever God commands is good; whatever God forbids is bad. Honesty is good *because* God commands it; hatred is bad *because* God forbids it. If God commanded us to hate one another then hatred would be good. If God forbade us to be truthful then honesty would be bad. At least, that's the opinion of the medieval philosopher William of Ockham (1285–1347).

The Euthyphro problem

Does God command us to do certain things because they are, in themselves, good? Or are certain things good by virtue of the fact that God commands them? Plato posed these questions (or, at least, something very like them) in his dialogue the *Euthyphro*, and they have been hotly debated by philosophers and theologians ever since.

Most people opt for the first of the two alternatives: namely that God commands certain things because they are good. Otherwise goodness appears to be arbitrary; dependent upon the whims of the Almighty. Indeed, it is hard to imagine anyone plumping for the second alternative: that things are good merely *because* God commands them. And yet a number of philosophers, most notably the English Franciscan friar, William of Ockham, have done so.

Ockham and Divine freedom

William of Ockham was a controversial figure. He was once charged with heresy, and was excommunicated by Pope John XXII following a row over the issue of Franciscan poverty. But he was a very astute thinker who produced significant work on logic, physics and theology. He is best known today for his principle that 'entities must not be multiplied beyond necessity', which is known as Ockham's razor.

Ockham's take on the Euthyphro problem was characteristically controversial. God, he said, is omnipotent. In other words, He has the power to do anything. Since He is omnipotent, there can be no constraints of any kind upon Him. He is free to choose and to act without restriction. So although He has commanded honesty, kindness and the like, it was – and is – possible for Him to forbid them instead.

There are no external standards to which God must conform. His will establishes what is good and bad, and what is right and wrong. This view has the counter-intuitive and somewhat unpalatable consequence that God might have commanded us to murder and torture one another, in which case murdering and torturing would have been morally good. But Ockham accepted this as a necessary consequence of Divine omnipotence.

Goodness vs. freedom

Nowadays, the philosophical doctrine that nothing is good until God commands it goes by the name *divine command theory*. It is unacceptable to most of us because we feel sure that some things are simply right or wrong in themselves rather than by divine fiat. But Ockham's point is that if certain things were bad in themselves then God would be unable to command them. His power would be limited by His goodness. So He would not be omnipotent, after all.

Ockham's philosophical and theological predecessor St Thomas Aquinas had already given serious thought to this matter. He concluded that God can neither do nor command evil. Not because of any external constraints but because of His own nature. Being perfectly benevolent, He always does and commands only what is good.

Aquinas's approach attempted to preserve both God's goodness and His freedom. But Ockham rejected it. He insisted that God is *maximally* free. In other words, free to the highest possible degree. Free to do absolutely anything that does not involve a logical contradiction.

God is good?

A major problem with Ockham's theory is that if it is true it makes no sense to call either God or His commands good. To say that God is good merely amounts to saying that He is consistent; that He acts in accordance with His own commands. And to say that God's commands are good merely amounts to saying that His commands are His commands.

The novelist, academic and Christian apologist C. S. Lewis put this point eloquently in his essay, *The Poison of Subjectivism*: 'if good is to be *defined* as what God commands, then the goodness of God Himself is emptied of meaning and the commands of an omnipotent fiend would have the same claim on us as those of the "righteous Lord".'

◄ 7. TOTAL PERFECTION

◄ 13. BURN, BABY, BURN

31. DUTY CALLS! ►

28

THE BRAIN IN THE JAR

Here's a thought-experiment, much beloved by philosophy teachers. Imagine that an evil scientist has removed your brain, placed it into a vat of chemicals and hooked it up to a powerful computer. The computer sends electrical signals to your still-functioning brain such that you seem to have real-world experiences. The program it runs is very sophisticated, and simulates with perfect accuracy all of the sights, sounds, tastes, smells and tactile experiences of ordinary life. It creates an illusory but totally convincing interactive world.

In this virtual world you can go for walks, handle objects, eat and enjoy food, chat to your friends, make love to your spouse, read philosophy books and even take foreign holidays. At least, you *think* you can do those things. In reality, you're just a brain in jar.

So far so good. Now comes the interesting bit. Can you be

sure that this story, or something like it, isn't true? Do you have any way of knowing that you're *not* a brain in a jar?

An insoluble problem?

The brain-in-the-jar puzzle is a modern spin on a thought-experiment introduced to philosophy by René Descartes, in which he considered the possibility that all of his experiences may have been delusions foisted upon him by an 'evil genius', a demonic deceiver. It is popular with philosophy teachers because it is a great way to get students questioning the assumptions we ordinarily make about the causes of our experiences and about the nature and existence of the external world.

It is notoriously difficult, perhaps impossible, to prove that the brain-in-the-jar hypothesis is false. Why so? Well, because if it *were* true, all of our experiences would be just as they are. But if we can't prove that the brain-in-the-jar hypothesis is false, then it seems that we can't truly know anything about the external world. We can't even be sure that it exists.

Accounting for our experiences

Although it may be impossible to *prove* that there is an external world populated by material objects, many people consider this to be the simplest and most reasonable supposition by which to account for our sensory experiences. But not everyone agrees.

We saw in chapter 15 that George Berkeley felt he had good

reasons for denying the existence of material objects, and for claiming that only minds and their ideas exist. In Berkeley's universe, God plays a role not unlike the evil scientist in the brain-in-the-jar story, but on a far, far grander scale. To most people, Berkeley's ideas about the nature of reality seem pretty weird. But there's an even weirder option, namely *solipsism*.

Solipsism

Solipsism is the belief that only the self exists. If I am a solipsist, I believe that the world consists only of my mind and its contents. If you are a solipsist, you believe that the world contains only your mind and its contents. If we are both solipsists then solipsism is untrue and we are both wrong.

The hardcore solipsist regards rocks, houses, trees, books, hospitals, symphonies, scientific theories, iced doughnuts, Homer Simpson, friends, family and even her own body as existing only in her own consciousness. The world, as she understands it, consists of a single mind – her own – and its contents. There's nothing else. Not even a brain in a jar, an evil scientist, a demonic deceiver or God.

Solipsism is pretty comical, when you think about it. There's a wonderful old story about a university lecturer who spoke so well in favour of solipsism that some students stayed behind after class and declared themselves convinced by his arguments. 'That's great news', the lecturer enthused. 'One so rarely gets the chance to speak to fellow solipsists!'

Embracing solipsism

It is perhaps as difficult to disprove solipsism as it is to disprove the brain-in-the-jar hypothesis. But is there any reason why you might actually *become* a solipsist? Well, let's say you were convinced by the brain-in-the-jar puzzle that all you really know is the contents of your own mind. In that case, if you were to limit your assent to whatever you indubitably know, you would be a solipsist.

Descartes once wrote: 'One cannot conceive anything so strange and so implausible that it has not already been said by one philosopher or another.' But solipsism is so strange and implausible a theory that it is an exception to the rule . . . or is it?

Although no great philosopher has been a solipsist, at least one great philosopher was acquainted with one. Bertrand Russell, in his book, *Human Knowledge: Its Scope and Its Limits*, tells us: 'I once received a letter from an eminent logician, Mrs Christine Ladd Franklin, saying that she was a solipsist, and was surprised there were no others. Coming from a logician and a solipsist, her surprise surprised me.'

9. ORANGES AREN'T ORANGE

15. ALL IN THE MIND

29

HARRY POTTER EXISTS

Harry Potter exists. Here's the proof. Think about the statement 'Harry Potter doesn't exist'. What's it about? Clearly, it's about Harry Potter. But a statement can only be *about* something if there's a *something* for it to be about. Therefore the statement 'Harry Potter doesn't exist' is self-refuting and Harry Potter exists.

You may object that the statement 'Harry Potter doesn't exist' isn't about Harry Potter at all; that it isn't about anything. But if it isn't *about* anything then it doesn't *say* anything. And clearly it *does* say something. So it must be about something – Harry Potter – after all.

You might try a different tack, and say that yes, the statement *is* about something, namely Harry Potter. But it isn't about a flesh-and-blood boy-wizard. Rather, it's about the *idea* of Harry Potter. But, in that case, the statement 'Harry Potter doesn't exist' is clearly false because, as an idea, Harry Potter certainly does exist.

So it is never true to say that Harry Potter doesn't exist. Therefore Harry Potter exists.

Square circles and Santa Claus

That was a none-too-serious way to introduce a serious philosophical issue: the problem of *negative existentials*.

A negative existential is a statement that denies the existence of something. Examples include 'Harry Potter doesn't exist', 'There is no Santa Claus', 'The square circle doesn't exist' and 'There's no largest prime number'. Since ancient times, statements like these have been the cause of much head-scratching amongst philosophers because although it seems obvious that some of them are true, upon reflection it can appear that none of them are true.

The problem is that in order to say that something doesn't exist you have to make a statement about it. You have to refer to it. But you can't refer to something that doesn't exist. So in the very act of denying its existence, you appear to confirm that it does exist.

Existence and subsistence

The Austrian philosopher Alexius Meinong (1853–1920) proposed a theory of objects which purported to shed some light on the problem of negative existentials. He suggested that some objects which do not exist nonetheless have a kind of being. Such objects *subsist* rather than *exist*.

Let's flesh those concepts out a bit. According to Meinong, the following objects all have being: chairs, trees, rocks, the tallest man in the world, the smallest prime number, 'the golden mountain' and Harry Potter. But they don't all have the same kind of being. The first four objects have actual spatiotemporal being. They exist. The remaining three objects have a non-spatiotemporal kind of being. They subsist. All objects, whether they exist or subsist, have certain characteristics. This means that we make true statements about them. For example, 'the tallest man in the world is tall'; 'the smallest prime number is even'; and so on.

Meinong's theory provides a nice easy solution to the problem of negative existentials. Consider again the statement 'Harry Potter doesn't exist'. What does it refer to? It refers to the *object* Harry Potter. What does it say about this object? That it doesn't exist. This is straightforwardly true. The object Harry Potter doesn't exist; it subsists.

It's worth noting that Meinong also claimed there are objects that neither exist nor subsist. The square circle, for example. Like all objects, the square circle has characteristics. You can make true statements about it such as 'the square circle is square' and 'the square circle is circular'. But these characteristics are contradictory. Therefore it is an impossible object and has no being.

Russell's refutation

Meinong's theory of objects is tremendous fun and was popular for a while, but was eventually knocked off its pedestal by the English philosopher and logician Bertrand Russell.

Russell said that when thinkers like Meinong postulate some kind of being to unicorns, golden mountains or, in our case, Harry Potter, they are being misled by grammar. They think that because we can make true propositions about such things then they must have some kind of logical being.

But, by Russell's account, 'Harry Potter' doesn't refer to some kind of entity; some kind of non-spatiotemporal being. Instead, it functions as a description. The statement 'Harry Potter exists' means that there is a thing (and only one thing) that is a boy-wizard, is marked by a lightning-shaped scar, attends Hogwarts School, owns an owl called Hedwig, etc., etc.

By the same token, the statement 'Harry Potter doesn't exist' means that there is no thing that answers to the description of being a boy-wizard, having a lightning-shaped scar, etc., etc. This statement is straightforwardly true since nothing in the real world *does* answer to that description.

So, according to Russell, Harry Potter doesn't exist – or even subsist – after all.

 5. NOTHING CHANGES

36. WORLD 3

NO ONE'S TO BLAME

Picture the following scenario. Christine drives home from work one evening and in a moment of inattention runs a red light. Fortunately, the road is clear and no one is hurt. Later that evening, Margaret drives home from work and in a moment of inattention runs a red light. Unfortunately, an elderly gentleman is crossing the road at the same time. Margaret's vehicle runs him over and kills him.

Now ask yourself the following questions. Is Margaret a worse person than Christine? Are her actions more blameable?

Moral luck

Put like that, both questions are likely to elicit a negative response. Most of us feel that the application of praise or blame ought to depend only on the content of people's actions and not on any accidental outcomes. Christine and Margaret are guilty of the same fault. Therefore they are equally to blame and, in this respect, have equal moral standing.

In practice, however, the outcomes of people's actions strongly influence the way we judge them, even when those outcomes are largely due to chance. Despite our moral intuitions to the contrary, we will, in fact, judge 'unlucky' Margaret far more harshly than 'lucky' Christine.

The present-day American philosopher Thomas Nagel makes use of the term 'moral luck' in describing situations of this kind. Moral luck occurs whenever praise or blame is applied to someone for an action or its consequences even though it is clear that the action or its consequences were largely outside their control.

Nagel considers moral luck to be a perplexing, even paradoxical, phenomenon. On the one hand it seems irrational to dispense credit or blame for matters over which a person has no control. But, on the other hand, we do so.

Types of moral luck

The more you think about it, the larger the part that luck seems to play in things for which we are morally judged.

First, there's *constitutive luck*. This has to do with one's innate character or personality. Some people seem to be born with kindly and sympathetic natures; others seem naturally cold and selfish. But no one chooses the character they're born with. So ultimately one's constitution is a matter of luck.

Second, there's *circumstantial luck*. In part, this has to do with being in the right place at the right time, or being in the wrong place at the wrong time. Nagel gives the example of ordinary citizens of Nazi Germany who had to choose whether to oppose the regime or to 'behave badly'. 'Most of them', he writes, 'are culpable for having failed the test'. Citizens of other countries may well have behaved just as badly in similar circumstances, but luckily for them their circumstances were different and so they did not. They, therefore, are not culpable.

Another aspect of circumstantial luck has to do with the results of one's actions, in the sense of whether things turn out fortuitously or not. Returning to the earlier example, Christine and Margaret committed precisely the same driving offence, yet Margaret is judged – and will be punished – far more harshly than Christine.

Praise and blame

It is possible to argue that luck determines *all* of our actions. Here's how. Our characters are shaped by two forces: nature and nurture. Nature is a matter of constitutive luck while nurture is a matter of circumstantial luck. So our characters are determined by luck. Now, the actions we perform are determined by our characters and by external circumstances. Both of these are down to luck. So everything we do is ultimately determined by factors that we do not control.

But if this is true, how can we blame people for their actions? It seems plainly wrong to blame people for things that are beyond their control. So it seems wrong to praise or blame them for *anything*.

This doesn't mean that we can't celebrate or deplore what people do. We can admire certain actions and find certain others distasteful. But if luck determines all that we do, we seem driven to conclude that no one is blameable for anything.

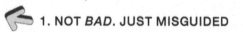 **1. NOT *BAD*. JUST MISGUIDED**

31

DUTY CALLS!

Imagine you are sitting at home watching TV. An advert comes on asking you to donate money to help the victims of a natural disaster. You see pictures of devastated homes, distraught men and women, and crying children. Moved by this, you pull out your credit card and make a sizeable contribution. Have you acted morally?

Surely, the answer is yes. Prompted by feelings of compassion, you have given generously to help the needy and unfortunate. Isn't this an example *par excellence* of a moral action? Not according to Immanuel Kant, it isn't. By his account, acts of compassion are not necessarily moral, and acts performed *purely* out of compassion have no moral worth at all.

The grounding of morals

In the *Groundwork of the Metaphysics of Morals*, Kant sought to discover the fundamental principle underpinning morality.

Rather than asking what such-and-such a person ought to do in such-and-such circumstances, he asked, what is the standard by which all actions, of all agents, in all circumstances are to be judged?

For example, we can be said to know that people ought to keep their promises. But *how* do we know? It can't be something we learn from experience: by observing how people do, in fact, behave. Because even if lots of people were seen to break their promises it would still be the case that they *ought* to keep them.

But if moral judgements aren't empirically grounded, where are they grounded? Kant's answer is that they must be grounded in reason. He wrote: 'the basis of obligation must not be sought in human nature or in the circumstances of the world in which [man] is placed, but . . . simply in the concepts of pure reason.'

Good will

Kant began his investigation with the observation, 'It is impossible to conceive of anything in the world, or indeed out of it, which can be called good without qualification save only a good will.'

There are many things that we might call 'good': wealth, generosity, courage, intelligence, good looks, etc. However, all of these things can be used to serve bad or evil ends. Therefore none of them is an unqualified good. There is, in fact, only one unqualified good, namely a good will.

A good will is good even when it does not succeed in

fulfilling its purpose. We may will a good action which circumstances prevent us from performing. Nonetheless our will itself is good. Or we may will a good action which turns out to have unforeseen injurious effects. Nonetheless our will itself is good.

According to Kant, we can be held accountable for the orientation of our wills in a way that we cannot be held accountable for our dispositions, our emotional reactions or our circumstances. Therefore it is our wills that are central to morality.

Acting for duty's sake

What, then, *is* a good will? Kant's answer is that a good will is one that acts for the sake of duty.

Here Kant stressed that to be deemed good a will must act not merely in accordance with duty, but explicitly for duty's sake. He illustrated this by means of an example. A tradesman who refrains from overcharging his customers acts *in accordance with duty*. In other words, he acts the way duty would prescribe. But he may do so simply because he thinks it's good for business, or because he doesn't want to get into trouble. But in that case, he is not acting *for duty's sake*; he's not charging his customers fairly simply because it's the right thing to do.

Kant said that a will is good only when it acts out of duty; and that an action is morally good only when it is done for duty's sake. This is a surprising notion, as the following example will show. Imagine that two people, Mike and Sue, take turns visiting their elderly housebound uncle. Mike is a naturally kind-hearted person who visits because he can't bear to think of his uncle sitting lonely and alone. Sue is not so tender-hearted and would really rather not visit, but she goes anyway because she thinks it's something she ought to do.

Kant would say that in this situation only Sue acts morally. Mike acts the way he does merely because it's in his nature to be kind. He acts out of inclination. But Sue acts the way she does out of a motive of duty.

Just to be clear, Kant isn't saying that Mike acts wrongly. He's just saying that Mike's actions, in this case, are not morally praiseworthy.

To many people this notion of morality divorced from emotion seems plainly wrong. They argue that certain emotions such as compassion and generosity have intrinsic moral worth. But a very positive feature of Kant's theory is that it makes morality possible for those who are not by nature kind, compassionate or generous. On Kant's view, anyone who is capable of understanding where their duty lies can be a good person.

What *is* our duty?

In closing, a word ought to be said about Kant's conception of duty. It's all very well saying we ought to do our duty. But what does that mean?

Very briefly, Kant thought that as rational beings we have certain duties. These duties are *categorical*. In other words, they are absolute and unconditional; they apply at all times and in all circumstances. Morality consists of a system of categorical duties such as: do not lie, do not break your promises, etc. But these are all derived from one basic principle, the so-called *categorical imperative*.

Kant expressed the categorical imperative in a variety of ways. One version says 'act only according to that maxim whereby you can at the same time will that it should become a universal law'. Another version says we should treat others as 'ends in themselves and not as means only'.

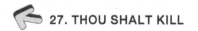 **27. THOU SHALT KILL**

40. RULES . . . RULES . . . RULES . . .

32

MIND YOUR BEHAVIOUR

If you were told that a certain person is 'afraid of spiders', what would you take that to mean? Well, you would probably interpret it to mean that spiders put them in an anxious state of mind; that whenever they see or think about eight-legged web-spinning creatures they have an unpleasant inner experience. And you would most likely associate that state of mind with certain behaviours, such as shuddering, running around and screaming.

The English philosopher Gilbert Ryle (1900–76) would interpret it differently. For him, being afraid of spiders has nothing to do with states of mind or inner experiences. It is purely about being disposed to behave in certain ways, where spiders are concerned.

Ryle was a *behaviourist*. A behaviourist, in the philosophical sense of the term, is someone who denies the existence of the mind; who claims that all descriptions of the mind and mental states turn out, upon analysis, to be nothing more than descriptions of people's actual or potential behaviour.

No ghost in the machine

People typically think of human beings (and perhaps certain animals) as being different from other objects in nature. Items such as rocks, tables, trees, stars and electrons are thought to be purely material objects, which operate solely under the influence of physical laws. Human beings, on the other hand, are considered to have something extra: a mysterious, immaterial entity known as the mind.

The mind is considered to be the source and repository of all our thoughts, feelings, desires, emotions and volitions. These inner states are thought to be entirely private; known only to the individual to whom the mind belongs.

But Ryle described this dualist view of human beings as 'a big mistake'. In his most famous work, *The Concept of Mind*, he disparagingly referred to it as 'the dogma of the Ghost in the Machine'.

Mind is behaviour

Behaviourists maintain that every statement we can make about mental states can, in principle, be translated into statements about actual or potential behaviour. So the statement 'John is in pain' is really just a shorthand way of saying that John is wincing, moaning and groaning, and subject to nerve impulses of certain sorts. Similarly, 'John is happy' is just a shorthand way of saying that he currently has a tendency to smile a lot and whistle jaunty tunes.

By this account, John's mind isn't something that exists above and beyond his behaviour. His mind doesn't *cause* his behaviour. His mind *is* his behaviour. There's no more to a person's mental states than the behaviour he exhibits or is disposed to exhibit.

An analogy

Ryle illustrated this strange-seeming concept by means of an analogy. Imagine that a foreign visitor takes a tour of Oxford University. He visits Balliol College, the Bodleian Library, the various laboratories and lecture halls, the Ashmolean Museum and so forth. At the end he says, 'That was very interesting, but I still haven't seen the University!' We make the same error, Ryle insisted, when we look at someone's behaviour, at the purposeful, intelligent activities they engage in, and then seek for something else – the 'mind' – orchestrating it all.

A person's behaviour doesn't provide clues to the workings of some mysterious, ghostly mind any more than the behaviour of a planet, a tree or an electron does. A person's behaviour *is* his mind, and is as fully open to public scrutiny as the workings of the planet, the tree and the electron.

Ryle wrote: 'Overt intelligent performances are not clues to the workings of minds; they *are* those workings.'

Two objections: one devastating

Behaviourism, if true, blows the mind-body problem right out of the water. There's no need to account for the way in which the mind influences behaviour because mind *is* behaviour. But *is* behaviourism true?

One common criticism is that behaviourism fails to distinguish between actually experiencing and merely pretending to experience mental states. It's one thing for John to be in pain, and quite another thing for him to pretend to be in pain. But since in both cases John winces, cries out and so on, the behaviourist must regard both states as identical.

This criticism is easily dealt with. Despite surface similarities there are plenty of observable differences between being in pain and merely pretending to be so. Not even the most skilled actor could produce the changes in blood pressure, heart rate, respiration and body temperature that accompany genuine pain. The behaviour he exhibits would therefore represent his true mental state: that of mimicking pain.

A more damning, indeed devastating, criticism of behaviourism is that although it seems to work quite well when applied to other people's mental states, it fails dismally when applied to our own. For example, when I say 'I am in pain' I don't simply mean that I am wincing, moaning and groaning, and so on. I mean that I am actually *feeling* pain. The behaviourist account ignores an essential aspect of pain: it hurts!

If behaviourism were true we would need to observe our own behaviour in order to know our own minds. But we know what we are thinking or feeling without having to do this. We have direct access to our own mental states. A classic philosophical joke makes this point nicely: *Two behaviourists have sex. Afterwards one turns to the other and says, 'Wow! That was great for you. How was it for me?'*

 **18. THE GHOST IN THE MACHINE**

33

BODY-SWAPPING

Imagine that, one night, the soul of a prince, with all of his princely thoughts, enters the body of a cobbler. Who is it next morning that wakes up in the cobbler's pyjamas? The English philosopher John Locke (1632–1704), who first posed this question, said that the *man* who wakes up is the cobbler, but the *person* who wakes up is the prince.

Locke discussed the body-swapping prince in *An Essay Concerning Human Understanding* where it appears as part of a discussion of personal identity. In philosophy, the problem of personal identity concerns questions about how people retain their identity over time. For example, what makes the balding middle-aged man I am now the same person as the hirsute young man I used to be?

Grains of sand and oak trees

Locke laid the groundwork for his discussion of personal identity with a preliminary discussion about the identity of non-living and living things. He said that the identity of non-living things depends entirely upon their material constitution. For example, a grain of sand remains the same grain of sand just as long as it is constituted from the same atoms. This means that if one atom is taken away it is no longer the same grain of sand.

The case is different for living things. Locke said that their identity depends not on their material constitution, which is constantly changing, but on their functional organisation: 'on the continuation of the same life'. An oak tree growing from a small plant to a gigantic tree remains the same oak because of the continued function of its living parts. Similarly for a colt growing into a horse.

Man and person

When it comes to the identity of human beings, Locke distinguished between the terms *man* and *person*. By 'man' Locke meant a living organised body of a certain kind whose identity, like that of other living things, is bound up with the continuation of the same life. 'The identity of man . . . consists . . . in nothing but a participation of the same continued life, by constantly fleeting particles of matter, in succession vitally united to the same organised body.'

By 'person', on the other hand, Locke meant 'a thinking intelligent being, that has reason and reflection, and can consider itself as itself, the same thinking thing, in different times and places.' The identity of a person is therefore bound up with consciousness or psychological continuity.

So, on Locke's account, the identity conditions for a man are not at all the same as the identity conditions for a person. The identity conditions for a man have to do with the body; whereas the identity conditions for a person have to do with consciousness.

Weird consequences

Locke's theory of personal identity has some very interesting consequences. For example, if by some accident every memory of my past life were erased then I would remain the same man that I am now but I would no longer be the same person.

More bizarrely, if my consciousness were somehow transferred to the brain of a pig, or to a computer, then that pig, or that computer, would become the person that I am now. More bizarrely still, if my consciousness were transferred simultaneously to the brains of *two* pigs, then both pigs would become the person that I am now (since both of their consciousnesses would be continuous with mine).

These scenarios are, obviously, rather fanciful. But Locke wouldn't have considered them unimportant. In fact, he spent a lot of time thinking about hypothetical situations that are just as weird. For example, the case of the prince and the cobbler, previously described.

Why bother?

Locke has a reputation as a commonsense philosopher. So one might wonder why he was so interested in the distinction between *man* and *person*; and why he troubled himself with such bizarre thought-experiments. Well, mainly, it's because he wanted to show that personal immortality is possible. He wanted to show that it is possible for us, on Resurrection Day, to rise again in new and different bodies – and yet still be *us*.

6. NOTHING STAYS THE SAME

34. CANNIBAL CONUNDRUMS

CANNIBAL CONUNDRUMS

St Thomas Aquinas (1225–74) is widely regarded as the greatest of the medieval philosophers. He combined exceptional acuteness as a thinker with deep reverence for the scriptures; and held that true faith and right reasoning can never be opposed to one another. Accordingly, he took great pains to resolve any apparent contradictions between faith and reason – no matter how trivial and obscure.

St Raymond of Pennafort once asked him to prepare a defence of the Christian faith to be used in debate against infidels and unbelievers. Aquinas produced the *Summa contra Gentiles*: a kind of theological manual for missionaries, which employed meticulous philosophical analysis to lend support to the revealed truths of Christianity. Amongst the hundreds of topics discussed in this vast work is a detailed discussion of cannibalism. Not, as you might imagine, because Aquinas felt that missionaries needed advice on how to avoid being eaten, but rather because of a tricky theological problem relating to the resurrection.

The resurrected missionary

Consider the following scenario. A missionary is eaten by a cannibal. Many years later, the final trumpet sounds and the dead rise for the Last Judgement. Ordinarily, bodily resurrection presents no difficulties to the Almighty. He simply reassembles each person using original material, albeit perhaps by now scattered across the globe. But what about the flesh the cannibal acquired by eating the missionary? To whom will it be restored?

The problem seems trite to us. But for Aquinas it was of the utmost importance since 'the resurrection would surely not be universal and entire, if each one did not regain what he had before'. His judgement on the matter is that the missionary has nothing to worry about: 'the flesh consumed will rise again in the man in whom it was first perfected by a rational soul'.

The resurrected cannibal

But what of the cannibal? How will *he* be resurrected? Aquinas, with characteristic thoroughness, considered two cases: (1) the cannibal who has eaten other food besides human flesh, and (2) the cannibal who has eaten only human flesh.

Aquinas said that in case (1) the cannibal 'will rise again with only such matter as he acquired from . . . other food'. This means that there will be parts missing from his resurrection body, but God will make up the deficiency. In case (2) the cannibal will 'rise again with what he received from his parents' and once again 'the deficiency will be supplied by the omnipotence of his Creator'. The thought here seems to be that only the flesh the thoroughgoing cannibal acquired during conception or in the womb is truly his own.

The resurrected second-generation cannibal

Having dealt satisfactorily with the resurrection of both cannibal and victim, Aquinas turned his attention to one final – and especially knotty – problem. What becomes of a cannibal who has eaten only human flesh, and whose *parents* have eaten only human flesh? This is similar to case (2) above, but with an added complication. The bodily material that he received from his parents was not strictly theirs to give.

Aquinas said that the second-generation cannibal will rise with the flesh he received from his parents, even though ultimately it derives from their victims. This leaves the victims short of bodily material, but not to worry: 'he whose flesh was consumed will be supplied from another source'.

Unsatisfying

Although commendably thorough, Aquinas's solution of the cannibal conundrum is messy and unsatisfying. The resurrection seems to require a complex – and, it must be said, somewhat arbitrary – swapping and changing of flesh. Plus, in every case there are deficits which God must make good using non-original material.

Aquinas didn't view the non-original material as a problem. He wrote: 'there is no need that whatever was in man materially should rise again in him; and . . . if anything be lacking, it can be supplied by God's power'. But if that's the case, why did he worry about the problem at all? Why was he so concerned for everyone to retain at least some part of their original body?

The answer is that he didn't believe the identity of a person can be preserved unless there is at least *some* physical continuity. Therefore a certain bare minimum of original material must survive in the resurrection body. It is this requirement that causes all the difficulties.

The prince and the cobbler revisited

Aquinas was by no means the only philosopher who worried about the resurrection of cannibals. St Augustine discussed the identical problem (and came to similar conclusions) almost a millennium earlier. In the seventeenth century, John Locke gave some thought to the matter. He maintained that his analysis of personal identity in the case of the body-swapping prince and cobbler holds the solution to the cannibal conundrum. Why so? Because it shows that it is possible for someone to be resurrected with an entirely different body, and yet remain precisely the same person.

← 6. NOTHING STAYS THE SAME

← 33. BODY-SWAPPING

39. THE ULTIMATE VICE →

35

PHILOSOPHY? NONSENSE!

In *An Enquiry Concerning Human Understanding*, David Hume conducted a detailed investigation into the kinds of things we can know and the methods by which we can come to know them.

One of his most startling and compelling conclusions is that a great deal of philosophy is nonsense. For more than two thousand years, the likes of Plato, Augustine, Aquinas and Leibniz have made weighty pronouncements about God, the human soul, absolute moral values and so forth. But it is all hot air. Bunkum. Or, in Hume's words, 'sophistry and illusion'.

Two fields of enquiry

Hume argued that there are only two valid objects of human reason; two proper fields of human enquiry. He labelled them *Relations of Ideas* and *Matters of Fact*.

The sciences of geometry, algebra and arithmetic are concerned with Relations of Ideas. The knowledge we derive from them is intuitively or demonstrably certain, and can be discovered by the mere operation of thought. Take for example, Pythagoras' Theorem which states that in a right-angled triangle the square of the hypotenuse is equal to the sum of the squares of the remaining sides. This expresses a relationship between the terms *triangle*, *right angle* and *hypotenuse*, and can be conclusively demonstrated to anyone who fully grasps the meanings of those terms.

Disciplines such as physics, chemistry, history and geography, on the other hand, are concerned with Matters of Fact. The knowledge we gain from them comes through experience; through investigating how things actually are in the world; and it is never entirely certain. Take, for example, a statement from physics: 'unlike magnetic poles attract one another'. We know that this statement is true because we have constantly observed that unlike poles do, in fact, attract one another. But this knowledge falls short of absolute certainty since it is conceivable that on a future occasion unlike poles may repel one another. We can't demonstrate that this rule *must always* hold true; we can only note that so far it *always has* held true.

Hume's Fork

Hume's reasoning here seems pretty straightforward and uncontroversial. But he proceeded to make powerful – indeed, devastating – use of it.

There are, he said, only two valid objects of human reason: Relations of Ideas and Matters of Fact. This means that when we are presented with any putative item of knowledge we can ask ourselves:

1. is it derived from a demonstrably certain relation of ideas? and

2. is it a matter of empirical fact, confirmed by experience?

If neither of these questions can be answered in the affirmative, then the supposed item of knowledge isn't really knowledge at all.

This simple yet powerful principle is often labelled Hume's Fork. But it could equally well be labelled Hume's Knife because it can be used to slice through so much baloney. If we accept it as a legitimate principle we must dismiss many celebrated philosophical ideas, including many of those discussed in this book. All lofty pronouncements regarding the nature of God, the afterlife, the human soul and so on must be rejected as clever-sounding nonsense.

Why? Because such things are not valid objects of enquiry. We cannot know or learn anything about them. They cannot be investigated using the kind of abstract reasoning we find in books of logic or mathematics; nor can they be investigated by empirical observation or testing. Therefore they cannot be investigated at all.

Fairyland philosophy

Doubtlessly, the Platos, Augustines, Aquinases and Leibnizes of this world would repudiate Hume's charge. After all, even their most abstruse metaphysical theories are reached using a combination of abstract and empirical reasoning – employing, as it were, both prongs of Hume's Fork.

But Hume's retort would be that they use these methods without sufficient care and attention (and without sufficient intellectual modesty). The ideas they employ in their abstract reasonings are not clear and unambiguous like those employed in mathematics, and their empirical arguments are used to draw conclusions that go way beyond everyday experience.

For example, Hume was scathing about Malebranche's doctrine of occasionalism, which we met in chapter 19. Such a doctrine, he argued, could never carry conviction with anyone 'sufficiently apprized of the weakness of human reason, and the narrow limits to which it is confined'. In such cases: 'We are got into fairy land, long ere we have reached the last steps of our theory; and there we have no reason to trust our common methods of argument, or to think that our usual analogies and probabilities have any authority.'

 19. HOW DID THAT HAPPEN?

22. YOU CAN'T PREDICT THE FUTURE

37. NOTHING TO DISCUSS

36

WORLD 3

One of philosophy's most enduring puzzles is this: how many kinds of stuff are there? Some philosophers, *monists*, say there's only one kind of stuff. Materialists, for example, claim that everything is material while idealists claim that everything is mental. Other philosophers, *dualists*, say there are two kinds of stuff. Descartes, as we have seen, said there's both mind and matter.

The Austrian-born British philosopher Karl Popper (1902–94) was neither a monist nor a dualist, but rather a *pluralist*. He divided the world into three realms, which he labelled world 1, world 2 and world 3.

World 1 contains physical objects such as rocks, trees, stars and animals as well as less tangible stuff like forces, radiation and energy. World 2 is the mental or psychological world of thoughts, sensations, desires and other mental phenomena. Finally, there's world 3. This contains the products of the human mind including languages, stories, scientific theories, ethical values, songs, symphonies, paintings and so on. They are all, by Popper's account, real. That is to say, they exist.

Thought processes and their products

There's an important distinction, Popper said, between 'the world of thought-processes, and the world of the products of thought processes'.

For example, I may study and try to understand Einstein's Special Theory of Relativity. In doing so, I engage in various thought processes. Eventually, I may come to grasp it. This thing, the 'it' that I grasp, is a not a thought process but rather a product of thought processes.

Thought processes are subjective. So the way you understand and conceptualise Einstein's theory may differ from mine. But this doesn't matter greatly. What really matters is the *content* of the theory in a logical sense, and this is not subjective. It is something that we examine, discuss, agree upon, argue about and criticise.

Thought processes are world 2 objects, and are subjective. But the products of thought processes are world 3 objects, and are objective.

Beethoven's Fifth

Beethoven's Fifth Symphony is another creation of the human mind and therefore a world 3 object. Like many other world 3 objects, it is embodied in a number of world 1 objects, such as musical scores, CD recordings, memory impressions in musicians' brains, etc. It is, therefore, an abstract world 3 object which is embodied in various concrete world 1 objects.

The materialist disputes this. He says that the concrete objects exist but the abstract object doesn't. True, we often *speak* as though the Fifth Symphony were an existing thing, but ultimately the thing we call 'the Fifth Symphony' reduces to a set of concrete objects such as live performances and CD recordings.

The dualist agrees with the materialist as far as the concrete objects are concerned, but also insists upon the existence of various mental or psychological objects. For him, the subjective experiences of hearing, enjoying, anticipating and remembering the Fifth Symphony are also real. But, like the materialist, he denies that the Fifth Symphony itself exists, as such.

But Popper insisted that there is something to the Fifth Symphony over and above all of these physical and mental objects. When we say that the Fifth is a great symphony, we don't mean merely that lots of people have very positive mental responses to various written scores, CD recordings and live performances. We mean that there is a Fifth Symphony; and it is great. 'In that sense the World 3 object is a real ideal object, which exists, but exists nowhere, and whose existence is somehow the potentiality of its being interpreted by human minds.'

What makes world 3 objects real?

That's all very well and good. But none of it actually *proves* that world 3 objects are real. However, Popper had a positive argument up his sleeve; one which he regarded as decisive. We know that world 3 objects are real, he said, because they exert a causal effect upon physical things, i.e. upon world 1 objects.

Let's unpackage that thought. What does it mean to say that an object is real? Well, in the most primitive sense, we regard those things as real which we can touch and handle, i.e. everyday objects. We then extend this idea to include less tangible things like forces and radiation that can causally act upon or interact with ordinary material things.

Ultimately, then, we consider an object real if it can causally effect physical things. But, Popper argued, this is the case for world 3 objects. Scientific theories have an enormous influence upon the physical word. The special theory of relativity, for example, gave rise to the atom bomb. Ideologies too shape the physical world. Consider the impact that Greek myths and the American Constitution have had upon the human race, and, as a result, on the world around us.

It's true that world 3 objects lack the concreteness of ordinary material objects. But, Popper maintained, they're real nonetheless: 'real in a sense very much like the sense in which the physicalist would call physical forces, and fields of forces, real, or really existing'.

By Popper's account, then, the theory of evolution, the

Mona Lisa and the Bible are real world 3 objects; as are the French language, the series of natural numbers and The Beatles' *Sgt. Pepper* album.

To all of this, the critic may respond that it is not theories, ideologies and suchlike that affect the physical world but rather our grasp of them; that is, our mental states. These belong to world 2, not to world 3. Popper regarded this as an important objection, and conceded that world 3 objects affect world 1 objects only through the mediation of world 2 objects.

It has also been objected that the world 3 theory doesn't achieve much; that although there is no harm in calling creations of the human mind 'real' in a certain sense, there is little to be gained by it. The contemporary philosopher Peter Singer has pointed out that Popper did not use the world 3 theory to solve any major philosophical problems.

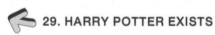

8. THE REAL WORLD

29. HARRY POTTER EXISTS

42. SCIENTIFICALLY UNPROVEN

37

NOTHING TO DISCUSS

According to the English philosopher A. J. Ayer (1910–89), you can't have a proper discussion about whether something is right or wrong. Why not? Because ethical statements are meaningless.

If someone tells you that sex before marriage is wrong, or that you ought to tell the truth, you can't, strictly speaking, disagree with them. You can't, strictly speaking, agree with them either. Because they're not actually *saying* anything.

The verification principle

Ayer's philosophical claim to fame was the introduction of logical positivism to the English-speaking world. Logical positivism was a twentieth-century movement associated with a group of thinkers known as the Vienna Circle.

The logical positivists claimed that there are two – and only two – ways of determining whether statements are true or not.

You can verify them by empirical observation, the way that scientists do. Or you can verify them by logical analysis, the way that mathematicians do. Statements that can't be verified either way are neither true nor false. They're meaningless.

Ayer and his fellow Vienna Circle-ites thus formulated what became known as the *verification principle*, which says that a statement is meaningful if and only if it is, in principle, verifiable.

The verification principle owes a lot to Hume's Fork, which we met in chapter 35. And, indeed, in good Humesian style, the logical positivists used the verification principle to dismiss a lot of traditional philosophical 'debates', especially metaphysical and theological ones, as empty drivel.

Ethical statements are meaningless

What about ethical statements? How does the verification principle apply to them? In his 1936 work, *Language, Truth, and Logic*, Ayer said that ethical statements are neither analytic (verifiable by logical analysis) nor empirically verifiable.

It is a feature of analytic statements that they cannot be denied without contradiction. Take, for example, a nice straightforward analytic statement like 'all bachelors are unmarried'. It would be nonsense to deny it since a bachelor is, by definition, unmarried.

You'd be contradicting yourself just as surely if you tried to deny that 'the sum of the internal angles of a triangle is equal to two right angles'. It takes a bit more brain-work and a more complex chain of reasoning to demonstrate that this is so. But so it is, nonetheless. (Check out Euclid's *Elements*, Book 1, Proposition 32, if you're not convinced.)

However, there's no contradiction involved in denying ethical statements. If you deny that 'you ought to tell the truth' or that 'sex before marriage is wrong' you may shock some people but you won't fall foul of the laws of logic. Therefore ethical statements are not analytic.

Ethical statements aren't empirically verifiable either. Close inspection of the world may reveal to you whether men and women are, in fact, truthful. But it will not reveal to you whether they *ought* to be so. Similarly, we cannot verify the truth of the statement 'sex before marriage is wrong' by examining whether people do or do not, in fact, have sex before they are married.

Expressions of emotion

Since ethical statements are neither analytically nor empirically verifiable they are, according to the verification principle, meaningless. They're not really statements at all, because they don't actually *say* anything. In that case, what *do* they do? Well, according to Ayer, they merely express emotions.

If someone says 'you ought to tell the truth' she is not making a factual statement. She is merely expressing an emotional response to the idea of telling the truth, and perhaps trying to elicit a similar emotional response in her listeners. She is, in effect, saying 'Truth-telling – hooray!' Similarly, when some-one says 'sex before marriage is wrong' all he is really saying is 'Pre-marital sex – boo!'

Ayer wrote: 'If a sentence makes no statement at all, there is obviously no sense in asking whether what it says is true or false. And we have seen that sentences which simply express moral judgements do not say anything.'

The view that ethical 'statements' are really expressions of emotion is known as *emotivism*. More colloquially, it goes by the name of Boo/Hooray theory.

But people *do* debate moral matters – don't they?

The emotivist claims that since ethical statements are meaningless it is impossible to have a genuine debate about a moral judgement. The obvious rejoinder is that people most certainly do have such discussions. And not just boo/hooray exchanges of feelings and emotions, but serious informed debates.

The emotivist's response is that meaningful discussion is certainly possible about factual issues. For example, if you approve of sex before marriage and I disapprove of it, we might enter into a meaningful discussion about how pre-marital sex, or the lack of it, affects individuals, couples and society at large. In doing so, we may even come to revise our feelings on the matter. But we can't meaningfully discuss the truth or falsity of the statement 'sex before marriage is wrong'. We can only express our emotional responses to it.

 31. DUTY CALLS!

 35. PHILOSOPHY? NONSENSE!

40. RULES . . . RULES . . . RULES . . . ➡

38

R.I.P. GOD

The German philosopher Friedrich Nietzsche (1844–1900) infamously declared that 'God is dead'. Taken at face value this is, of course, nonsense. The traditional Judeo-Christian conception of God is that of an all-powerful, unchanging being. Such a being cannot die. He exists forever, if He exists at all.

Nietzsche was well aware of this. In fact, when he first introduced the idea he put the words into the mouth of a madman who takes a lantern into the marketplace crying, 'I seek God! I seek God!' and then announces, 'God is dead. God remains dead. And we have killed him.'

Nietzsche knew, then, that his claim would strike readers as strange, even absurd. But that was the whole point. The statement 'God is dead' wasn't supposed to be taken literally. It was Nietzsche's striking and provocative way of saying that belief in God had outlived its usefulness to society.

The decline of religious belief

The statement 'God is dead' first crops up in Nietzsche's 1882 work, *The Gay Science*. Then it reappears as a central theme in his most popular work, *Thus Spoke Zarathustra*.

At that time, as the nineteenth century drew to a close, religious belief was on the wane in Western Europe. In an increasingly scientific and well-educated society, the unquestioning belief in God, the soul and an afterlife was no longer considered intellectually respectable. In announcing the death of God, Nietzsche was challenging his contemporaries to face up to this loss of faith and to think about its repercussions.

Despite its loss of faith, the society of Nietzsche's day still clung on to the same old moral values. But for Nietzsche the death of God meant the death of religious morality, specifically the Christian morality that had for so long dominated Europe. With God dead, Christian values were no longer valid. New ones were required.

Slaves and masters

Nietzsche wasn't at all sorry to see the decline in religious belief. He was fiercely critical of Christianity and its values.

By his account, Christianity had arisen among the slaves of the Roman Empire not because it embodied a true set of beliefs handed down from On High but because it fulfilled a psychological need. The slaves were powerless to liberate themselves from physical servitude, and so they used religion as a means of asserting spiritual and moral superiority over their masters. Christianity endorses slave-values such as pity, compassion and meekness, and rejects master-values such as self-interest, self-assertion and strength of will. Slaves are therefore seen as righteous, and masters as sinful.

Nietzsche claimed that Christianity was born out of weakness, fear and resentment. Furthermore, he regarded it as life-denying. It teaches that God is high, mighty and good; while we are lowly, weak and sinful. It encourages us to accept our lot in this life, and to place all of our hopes in the next. All of this was anathema to Nietzsche. In *Ecce Homo*, he wrote: 'The concept "God" was invented as the opposite of the concept "life" – everything detrimental, poisonous and slanderous, and all deadly hostility to life, was bound together in one horrible unit in Him!'

New values

For Nietzsche, then, the death of God was good news. It meant that people were free to choose their own values and shape their own destinies; to live for the here and now rather than the hereafter.

Nietzsche thought we ought to stop looking to God or anyone else for guidance. We should each of us live life on our own terms and express ourselves as individuals. This means shunning conformity, obedience and mediocrity, and living boldly and passionately.

The demise of God had paved the way for a new kind of morality. And it had paved the way for a new kind of individual: one who is powerful, non-conformist, optimistic, self-affirming, life-embracing and willing to create his own values. The ideal individual, who would embody all of these qualities, Nietzsche labelled the *Übermensch*, or 'superman'.

Alive and kicking?

But wasn't Nietzsche premature in announcing the death of God? After all, here we are, over a century later, and to all appearances God is still very much alive. Faith and religion are still powerful forces in the lives of millions upon millions of people, the world over.

Nietzsche, to an extent, seems to have anticipated this. In *Thus Spoke Zarathustra* he wrote: 'God is dead; but given the way of men, there will still be caves for thousands of years in which his shadow will be shown. And we – we still have to vanquish his shadow too.'

He would say, I think, that we are still coming to terms with the death of God.

Not so strange, after all

Nietzsche's claim that God is dead is intended to be strange-sounding and paradoxical. But it's really not so strange once you understand it. In using it, Nietzsche demonstrated his psychological astuteness and genius as a writer. Had he merely stated that belief in God is outdated his words might easily have been passed over or forgotten. But by coining the phrase 'God is dead' he captured the public imagination.

 7. TOTAL PERFECTION

14. AGAIN, AND AGAIN, AND AGAIN . . .

27. THOU SHALT KILL

39. THE ULTIMATE VICE

39

THE ULTIMATE VICE

Masturbation has a bad rep. The British slang-word 'wanker' literally means 'a person who masturbates'. But it is used – and used very frequently – as a general term of abuse. Such is the sense of furtiveness and sordidness surrounding masturbation that there are literally dozens of euphemisms and dysphemisms for it.

But how did masturbation get its bad rep? What could possibly be wrong with – to use one common euphemism – 'pleasuring yourself'? And, assuming that masturbation *is* wrong, just how wrong is it? How highly does it rank among the sins of the flesh?

St Thomas Aquinas, the greatest of the medieval philosophers, didn't baulk at these questions. In the *Summa Theologica*, he addressed them with characteristic thoroughness and intellectual rigour, and concluded that not only is masturbation bad, but it is very bad indeed. Worse even than rape.

What's wrong with wanking?

Aquinas argued that God has a purpose for everything in creation. Some of God's purposes are beyond our comprehension, but others lie within the limits of our understanding. The *natural law* is that part of the divine plan which we are able to grasp without special revelation. When we act in accordance with natural law we fulfil God's purposes.

Aquinas's views on human sexuality provide an excellent example of his natural law theory at work. According to him, the sexual act has three purposes: procreation, the strengthening of the marital bond and pleasure. Given this premise, it can be demonstrated that, for example, adultery is wrong because it destroys rather than strengthens the marital bond, and because any offspring resulting from an adulterous union will be reliant upon the care of a non-natural parent.

So what's wrong with masturbation? Well, it's wrong on two counts. First, it doesn't produce babies; and second, it doesn't promote closeness between husband and wife.

Masturbation is wrong, then. But *how* wrong?

Six varieties of lust

In the *Summa Theologica*, Aquinas said that 'the sin of lust consists in seeking venereal pleasure not in accordance with right reason'. This means seeking it by methods inconsistent with procreation; or seeking it through proper procreative sex but in inappropriate circumstances.

There are, in total, six categories of sexual sin. Aquinas listed them as 'simple fornication, adultery, incest, seduction, rape, and the unnatural vice'. The term *unnatural vice* is an umbrella term encompassing masturbation, homosexuality, bestiality and heterosexual acts such as anal and oral sex.

Now, the five categories of sin apart from unnatural vice are all 'sins against reason'. They involve performing the proper procreative sex-act but in the wrong circumstances or with the wrong people. The unnatural vices, on the other hand, are not only sins against reason but also 'sins against nature'. They involve improper sex-acts of a kind that cannot produce babies.

Unnatural vices are worst

The unnatural vices are doubly bad, then, which means that they're worse than fornication, adultery, incest, seduction and rape.

There is, of course, an obvious objection to all of this. Aquinas anticipated it, and expressed it like this: 'Now adultery, seduction and rape which are injurious to our neighbour are seemingly more contrary to the love of our neighbour, than unnatural sins, by which no other person is injured. Therefore the unnatural sin is not the greatest among the species of lust.' In other words, sins like masturbation harm no one but the sinner; whereas sins like adultery and rape harm other people as well. Surely, then, adultery and rape are worse than masturbation.

Aquinas replied that sins against nature injure not only the sinner himself or herself but also God. '[T]he order of nature is from God Himself:' he wrote, 'wherefore in sins contrary to nature . . . an injury is done to God, the Author of nature'.

Therefore, since sins against God are more heinous than sins against one's fellow man, unnatural vices such as masturbation and oral sex are worse than more 'natural' (!) vices such as incest, adultery and rape.

Injure God?

But this raises another objection. Simply this: how does one injure God? God is an all-powerful, unchanging being. In what sense, then, can He be harmed?

We saw in the last chapter that Nietzsche was fiercely critical of Christian morality. One of his many beefs with it was this notion that our sins can somehow injure God. He wrote: 'The Christian presupposes a powerful, overpowering being who enjoys revenge. His power is so great that nobody could possibly harm him, except for his honour.'

Nietzsche thought that this idea gives Christians a perverted sense of right and wrong. '[E]very deed is to be considered solely with respect to its supernatural consequences without regard for its natural consequences', he wrote.

It is the assumption that God can, in some sense, be harmed that led Aquinas to make the really quite shocking claim that masturbation is worse than rape. It seems a strange – and dangerous – assumption to make.

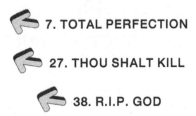 7. TOTAL PERFECTION

27. THOU SHALT KILL

38. R.I.P. GOD

40

RULES . . . RULES . . . RULES . . .

A number of great thinkers have formulated theories about how to live right. Often these are embodied in universal rules or codes: principles that are said to apply to everyone, everywhere and at all times. This sounds like a very good thing. After all, if everyone were to live their lives by a moral code — one rooted in justice and fairness — life would be great, wouldn't it?

Surprisingly, not everyone thinks so. Some philosophers have argued that adopting ethical codes is a bad thing; that it compromises your integrity.

What's wrong with rules?

What could possibly be wrong with living your life by a moral code? Well, critics say that the weakness of such systems is the very thing that is generally considered their strength, namely their universality and impartiality.

The trouble with rules, codes and systems is that they offer a one-size-fits-all approach to virtue. They operate on the assumption that what is right for one person must be right for another. But, in fact, each person is unique. So what is right for one person may *not* be right for another.

Ethical systems try to squeeze people into a mould. They promote ways of being and doing that take no account of individuality, and that therefore damage your integrity.

Here, it should be noted that the English word 'integrity' can be used in two very different senses. It can mean 'strict adherence to moral and ethical principles' or it can mean 'the state of being whole, entire or undiminished'. Clearly, conforming to ethical principles can't damage your integrity in the first sense of the word. But it can do so in the second sense of the word.

Ducks and cranes

The Chinese philosopher Chuang Tzu (369–286 BC) illustrated this point by contrasting two water-birds: the duck and the crane. The duck's squat body and short legs enable it to float on the water and dive beneath its surface. The crane's long neck and legs enable it to wade through the shallows foraging for food. Each bird gets along beautifully by acting in accordance with its own nature. It would be absurd to expect them to behave the same way.

Similarly, Chuang Tzu said, it is absurd to expect all human beings to conform to identical rules and principles. Everyone is different, and so everyone ought to behave differently. Strict adherence to external standards prevents you from expressing who you really are, and thus compromises your integrity; your wholeness.

But if codes and systems cannot appropriately guide individuals' behaviour, what can? ChuangTzu's answer to this question involves two very important concepts in Chinese thought: *Tao* and *Te*.

The Way and its power

ChuangTzu was aTaoist.Taoism is a system of thought founded around the same time as Confucianism by a sage known as Lao Tzu. The central concept of Taoism is *Tao* which translates as 'the Way'. The Tao is a mysterious principle; an unseen power which runs through everything and directs the course of nature. It is indefinable and incomprehensible.

The ancient Taoist text the *Tao Te Ching* says, 'The Tao that can be spoken of is not the true Tao.' But although the Tao is itself unknowable, Taoist philosophers agree that it produces all things and enables them to exist in all their variety. It endows all things with their individual natures, qualities and powers.The power of theTao, the principle that enables things to be what they are, is called *Te*.

All living things have their own Te, their own nature, energy or qualities, by which they maintain themselves, grow and flourish.

Act naturally

For the Taoist, virtuous living isn't about subduing your desires and conforming to external rules. Rather, it is about living naturally, in harmony with your individual nature and with the nature of the world around you. It is about living in accordance with the Tao and the Te.

Chuang Tzu taught that trying to live according to artificial, socially imposed rules is a recipe for disaster. It can only lead to suffering and evil. Living naturally, on the other hand, with regard to your own Te and with regard to the Te of everything around you, is the source of all happiness and well-being.

But how do you tap into your Te? The short answer is, by living naturally and simply; by not trying too hard; by listening to your inner voice and going with the flow. The Taoist way of living is about allowing yourself to be yourself rather than struggling to develop a certain way.

The typical Taoist – if that's not a contradiction in terms – isn't greedy, grasping or ambitious. She isn't pushy and aggressive. She eats when she's hungry, sleeps when she's tired and does everything in the simplest, most unassuming way possible.

Getting involved

The Taoist approach to ethics is very appealing. It seems to take all the struggle and stress out of living virtuously. However, critics say that it can lead to laziness and selfishness.

In the early days of Confucianism and Taoism, philosophers from the two schools often had disagreements on this very point. Confucius taught his followers that living ethically means conscientiously fulfilling your various functions within society. Accordingly, he had laid down very specific codes of behaviour for them to adopt in their roles as parents, children, marriage-partners, siblings, friends, rulers and subjects.

The Confucians felt that it was their duty to follow these rules and to work hard to improve society. The Taoists, on the other hand, tended to favour withdrawing from society altogether. The Confucian philosopher Mencius once criticised the Taoist philosopher Yang Chu by saying that he wouldn't so much as pluck a hair from his head to save the world.

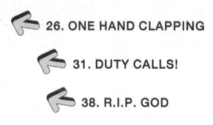

26. ONE HAND CLAPPING

31. DUTY CALLS!

38. R.I.P. GOD

41

ABSURD, BUT TRUE

Christian philosophers generally take great pains to demonstrate the reasonableness of their beliefs. As we have seen, Augustine, Aquinas, Anselm and the like constructed meticulous arguments to justify their ideas about the existence and nature of God.

But the Danish philosopher Søren Kierkegaard (1813–55) is an exception to the rule. Although a believer, he flatly denied that the existence of God and the truths of the Christian religion can be intellectually justified. More than that, he described the Christian message as 'absurd' and 'paradoxical'.

But this seems outrageous. Surely it makes no sense for someone to say, 'Oh, yes, I know my beliefs can't be justified. In fact, I know they're unreasonable. But I'm sticking to them anyway.'

So why *did* Kierkegaard believe? What prompted him to put faith in the absurd?

The 'absolute paradox'

Kierkegaard found fault with all of the standard philosophical arguments for the existence of God. For example, he viewed the ontological argument, which we met in chapter 7, as merely developing our conception of God rather than proving His actual existence. He also dismissed all attempts to justify Christianity on the basis of historical evidence. There are problems enough, he reasoned, with establishing the truth of ordinary historical events, never mind those as extraordinary as the incarnation.

In Kierkegaard's view, then, Christianity can be justified neither philosophically nor historically. But that is only half of the story. He also asserted that Christianity is inherently paradoxical and therefore positively *offensive* to reason.

The heart of the paradox lies in the incarnation: the doctrine that God became man. How can such a thing be? Kierkegaard asked. How can an infinite, eternal, unlimited God take on the form of finite, temporal, limited man? The very notion is absurd.

There's some debate over precisely what Kierkegaard meant when he described the incarnation as paradoxical. Some scholars interpret him as asserting that the concept of a *God-man* is a logical contradiction, like *married-bachelor* or *four-sided triangle*. Others interpret him as making the milder claim that *God-man* is a concept that defies our understanding; that offends our reason. Here I'll assume the latter, more defensible, interpretation.

The limits of human reason

According to Kierkegaard, human reason baulks at the very idea of the God-man. Our concept of God and our concept of man are such that we cannot unite them.

But perhaps the fault lies not with the concepts themselves but rather with our conceptual apparatus. Perhaps reason is simply not equipped to deal with God. This is, in fact, what Kierkegaard thought. Human reason, he argued, is too limited to grasp the incarnation. But sinfulness and pride prevent us from seeing and accepting this. We place arrogant faith in our powers of reason, and insist that since Christianity defies our comprehension it must be rejected.

The leap of faith

This being the case, how can we ever come to believe? This is where faith comes in. Through faith the believer sets aside his pride and acknowledges the limitations of human reason. He embraces the paradox.

The incarnation, then, is a paradox that can be embraced only through faith. But doesn't that make faith itself problematic? Given that it is the nature of fallen man to place arrogant confidence in his own rational powers, what can possibly prompt him to take the leap of faith?

The answer is: a miracle. Faith arises in the believer as the result of a direct encounter with God; by an act of divine grace.

It can arise no other way. Kierkegaard wrote: 'But in that case is not faith as paradoxical as the Paradox? Precisely so . . . Faith is itself a miracle, and all that holds true of the Paradox also holds true of faith'.

This is a surprising, indeed startling, doctrine. But it accords well with the words of St Paul: 'For by grace are ye saved through faith; and that not of yourselves: it is the gift of God' (Ephesians 2:8, King James Bible).

Postscript: did Kierkegaard *really* think this?

Many of Kierkegaard's works were written under pseudonyms such as Johannes Climacus, Hilarius Bookbinder and Constantin Constantius which he adopted to prevent readers from knowing whether the opinions expressed were his own, or whether he was merely offering them for consideration. This is an admirable strategy for keeping the reader on her toes and forcing her to think for herself. But it can also be a source of frustration.

The lines of thought explored in this chapter were presented in *Philosophical Fragments* and *Concluding Unscientific Postscript*. Both were written under the pseudonym Johannes Climacus, with Kierkegaard himself credited as 'editor'. The authorship suggests that we cannot assume the views are Kierkegaard's own, but the editorship suggests that perhaps we can. Slippery character, Kierkegaard.

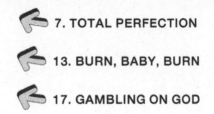

7. TOTAL PERFECTION

13. BURN, BABY, BURN

17. GAMBLING ON GOD

42

SCIENTIFICALLY UNPROVEN

Most people think (if they think about it at all) of scientific method as proceeding along the following lines. First, the scientist makes a large number of observations. Then she formulates a theory based on those observations. Then she subjects her theory to rigorous testing. If the theory survives those tests it is verified or confirmed.

For example, she may observe that acids and bases invariably react together to form a salt and water. From this she formulates the universal law 'the reaction of an acid with a base will always produce water plus a salt'. She then verifies her theory by observing the reactions of many different acids and bases, and checking that the law does indeed apply in every case.

The Austrian-born British philosopher Karl Popper (1902–94), in his 1934 work *The Logic of Scientific Discovery*, rejected this view. He argued that science does not and cannot proceed in this manner since no scientific theory ever *can* be verified.

To many people, this idea is astonishing. After all, you can pick up any science book and read about any number of thoroughly verified theories . . . can't you? Newton's theory of gravity, for example. That's a confirmed theory . . . isn't it?

Well, no on both counts, said Popper.

Science and induction

Every attempt at verifying a scientific theory is doomed to failure, Popper tells us, because of the problem of induction. As we saw in chapter 22, inductive arguments by their very nature cannot guarantee certainty. Therefore scientific laws can never be conclusively verified. For example, the argument:

1. Every ray of light that was ever observed travelled in a straight line. *Therefore*

2. All rays of light travel in straight lines.
isn't deductively valid. Even if the premise is true, the conclusion may not be.

Now, although scientific laws can't be conclusively verified, they most certainly can be conclusively *falsified*. This is because of an interesting and useful point of logic, namely that although no amount of confirming instances is sufficient to verify a universal law, a single non-confirming instance is sufficient to refute one. The argument:

1. A light ray was observed travelling along a curved path.
Therefore

2. Not all light rays travel in straight lines.
is deductively valid. If the premise is true then the conclusion must be true also.

According to Popper, then, science isn't about *confirming* theories and hypotheses. Rather it is about refuting or *falsifying* them. Science progresses by falsification rather than induction.

Falsificationism

Popper and his fellow *falsificationists* view science as progressing in the following manner. The scientist is presented with a problem: some aspect of the world that needs to be analysed or explained. She formulates a theory or hypothesis which seems to offer a solution, and then subjects it to rigorous testing in an attempt to refute it. If the theory survives those tests it can be accepted – but only provisionally.

In his excellent book, *What Is This Thing Called Science?* A. F. Chalmers sums it up nicely: 'It can never be said of a theory that it is true, however well it has withstood rigorous tests, but it can hopefully be said that a current theory is superior to its predecessors in the sense that it is able to withstand tests that falsified those predecessors.'

Newton's theory of gravity, for example, withstood rigorous testing for two centuries. But it was, nonetheless, eventually falsified. It was found to predict wrongly certain characteristics of the orbit of the planet Mercury. In due course it was replaced by Einstein's general theory of relativity, which successfully predicted the fine details of Mercury's orbit.

Since science progresses by falsification, it is essential that scientific theories are, in fact, falsifiable. The more falsifiable, the better. Theories that make bold, testable claims (and, needless to say, resist attempts to falsify them) are good theories. Theories which do not make testable claims, and are therefore not falsifiable, are not scientific theories at all.

Science and pseudoscience

For the falsificationist, the general theory of relativity is an example of a scientific theory *par excellence*. This geometric theory of gravitation was published by Albert Einstein in 1915. One of its predictions was that light beams would bend when travelling close to the sun. This was contrary to accepted laws of physics at the time, which stated that light always travels in straight lines. Einstein's novel prediction was spectacularly confirmed by astronomers during the total solar eclipse of 1919.

The triumph of the theory, which spawned newspaper headlines across the globe and catapulted Einstein to international stardom, impressed Popper immensely. After all, the prediction might just as conceivably *not* have been confirmed, in which case the theory would have been in ruins.

Popper was struck by the contrast between bold, testable theories like Einstein's and the vague, non-falsifiable theories of what he termed *pseudosciences* such as astrology. It is characteristic of pseudosciences to make predictions that are so vague as to be untestable (Popper gave the example of a newspaper horoscope reading 'Luck is possible in sporting speculation'). Similarly it is characteristic of the adherents of pseudosciences to embrace evidence that confirms their theories while ignoring evidence that falsifies them.

According to Popper, falsification is what sets scientific theories apart from pseudoscientific, religious and metaphysical theories. He wrote: 'One can sum up all this by saying that the criterion of *the scientific status of a theory is its falsifiability, or refutability, or testability.*'

Falsification falsified?

Popper's ideas about how science progresses have come in for some criticism. One such criticism is that he downplayed the role that confirmation plays in the advancement of science. After all, new theories receive a real boost when they make novel predictions that are subsequently *confirmed*. Consider, for example, the importance of the confirmation of Einstein's prediction that light waves will bend when travelling close to the sun.

Also, the history of science shows that there have been many occasions when scientists would have given up on important theories had they adhered rigorously to Popper's falsificationist method. For example, a consequence of Copernicus's Sun-centred model of the universe was that the apparent size of the planet Venus, as viewed from Earth, would vary markedly throughout the year. For reasons that were not then understood, observations made at the time did not bear this out. But despite this apparent falsification the theory was not abandoned. This was a very good thing since Copernicus's Sun-centred model was a big improvement on the earlier Earth-centred ones.

Neither of these criticisms, however, detracts from Popper's claim that while scientific theories can be conclusively falsified they can never be conclusively verified. No amount of confirmation can ever establish a theory as true.

 22. YOU CAN'T PREDICT THE FUTURE

36. WORLD 3

43

THE UNEXAMINED LIFE

The Greek philosopher Socrates famously declared that 'the unexamined life is not worth living'. What he meant by this is that everyone should spend time each day engaged in ethical discussion; that no one should live without subjecting their way of life to philosophical scrutiny.

This is a startling and provocative claim. After all, there are many things that seem to make life worthwhile: happiness, friends, family, religion, work and play – to name just a few. It seems absurd, and even rather annoying, for Socrates to suggest that unless a liberal dose of philosophising is added to the mix it's all worthless.

Two questions spring to mind. First, was he serious? Did he *really* believe that a life devoid of philosophy isn't worth living? And second, assuming that he *was* serious, why did he think it so absolutely necessary to examine one's life?

Socratic Method

Socrates had a very distinctive way of doing philosophy. He would stand in Athens' marketplace drawing passers-by into debate. His favourite ploy was to ask an acknowledged expert for his opinion on some matter. Then, by skilful questioning, he would demonstrate that the 'expert' didn't know so much after all. For example, he showed that an army general could give no satisfactory definition of courage and that a religious zealot could give no coherent account of what pleases God.

His intention wasn't to embarrass his opponents – though he frequently did. He was motivated by a desire for knowledge; and he believed that knowledge only emerges through a process of dialogue and systematic questioning.

Socrates on trial

Socrates made his famous claim that the unexamined life is not worth living while on trial for his life. His tricky questions had embarrassed and angered a number of Athens's most influential citizens. Consequently, in 399 BC he stood trial on a trumped-up charge of impiety and corrupting the young.

He conducted his own defence, and, eschewing the usual practice of flattering the jurors and appealing to their sympathy, he used the opportunity to make a robust defence of his way of life and to denounce Athenian democracy. Plato's *Apology* purports to be an account of the trial, and it is there

that we find the details of Socrates' speech, including his 'unexamined life' claim.

Socrates' mission

Socrates responded to the charge of impiety by informing the
jury that he had adopted his way of life by divine command:
'The god [Apollo] gave me a station, as I believed and understood, with orders to spend my life in philosophy and in examining myself and others.' His constant probing and questioning,
which so irritated his accusers, was therefore evidence of his
piety.

As regards the charge of corrupting the young, Socrates
responded that his lifestyle was virtuous and his influence ben-
eficial: '[T]he greatest good for a human being is to reason
every day about human excellence and the other things that
you hear me examining in conversation.'

As we saw in chapter 1, Socrates held that knowledge is
virtue; that once we truly know what is good, we will do it.
That was why he spent his days debating and arguing with his
fellow citizens. Because if together they could thrash out the
answers to his questions – if they could achieve true knowledge
of goodness, justice, courage, piety and the like – then virtue
would follow.

Understanding Socrates' claim

In claiming that the unexamined life is not worth living, Socrates wasn't dismissing the importance of the things we ordinarily take to be worthwhile: happiness, love, friends, family, religion, work, play and the like. His point was that if we are willing to examine our lives and values then together we can learn what human excellence is. Once we achieve this knowledge we will have everything we need to live well. Every aspect of our lives will improve.

But if, like Socrates' accusers, we refuse to examine ourselves then we will remain locked in ignorance. Our lives will lack virtue and every part of them will suffer. This is why Socrates tells the jurors, 'I go about doing nothing other than trying to persuade you, young and old, not to care for your bodies or your property more than, or even as much as, the excellence of your souls.'

 **1. NOT *BAD*. JUST MISGUIDED**

FURTHER READING

Chapter 1 Not *bad*. Just misguided

Who better to introduce you to Socrates than his star pupil, Plato? *The Last Days of Socrates* (Penguin Classics, 2010) contains four of Plato's dialogues (*Euthyphro*, *Apology*, *Crito* and *Phaedo*) tracking Socrates' trial, condemnation and death. All are beautifully written, compelling and packed full of first-rate philosophical discussion.

Socrates' views on the relationship between knowledge and virtue are explored in Plato's dialogue, *Protagoras*. This is available in *Protagoras and Meno* (Penguin Classics, new edn, 2005).

Chapter 2 Couldn't be better

Leibniz is one of history's great polymaths. *Leibniz* ('Past Masters', Oxford University Press, 1996) by George MacDonald Ross introduces his ideas on a whole raft of subjects, and is a fascinating read.

Modern Philosophy: The Seventeenth and Eighteenth Centuries ('Fundamentals of Philosophy', Routledge, 2003) by Richard Francks does a great job of explaining Leibniz's philosophical ideas to the general reader. Francks discusses Leibniz's claim that this is the best of all possible worlds in chapter 10.

Chapter 3 Couldn't be worse

Christopher Janaway's compact and informative *Schopenhauer: A Very Short Introduction* ('Very Short Introductions', Oxford University Press, 2002) is excellent. *Penguin Great Ideas: On the Suffering of the World* (Penguin, revised edn, 2004) is a pocket-sized collection of Schopenhauer's best essays and aphorisms. It's readable, insightful and – surprisingly, given the title – great fun.

Chapter 4 Selfish motives

James Rachels' *The Elements of Moral Philosophy* (McGraw-Hill, 4th edn, 2002) is an easy to read but intellectually stimulating introduction to ethics. Chapter 5 contains a detailed introduction to psychological egoism.

Chapter 5 Nothing changes

Chapter 3 of Roy Sorensen's *A Brief History of the Paradox: Philosophy and the Labyrinths of the Mind* (Oxford University Press

USA, new edn, 2005) provides an entertaining and stimulating introduction to Parmenides' ideas. It's also worth checking out chapter 2 of *Presocratic Philosophy: A Very Short Introduction* (Oxford University Press, 2004) by Catherine Osborne.

Chapter 6 Nothing stays the same

The First Philosophers: The Presocratics and Sophists (Oxford Paperbacks, 2009) by Robin Waterfield has a good chapter about Heraclitus. *Paradoxes from A to Z* (Routledge, 2nd edn, 2007) by Michael Clark has a brief but good section on the Ship of Theseus, and is a great resource for anyone interested in paradoxes generally.

Chapter 7 Total perfection

Brian Davies' *An Introduction to the Philosophy of Religion* (Oxford University Press, 3rd edn, 2003) covers all of the main arguments for the existence of God, including the ontological argument, very well. I also recommend *Introducing the Philosophy of Religion* (Routledge, 2009) by Chad Meister. Anselm's ontological argument can be found in his *Proslogion*. This is available in *Anselm of Canterbury: The Major Works* (Oxford University Press, reissue edn, 2008), which also includes Gaunilo's objections to the ontological argument and Anselm's reply. Descartes's *Meditations on First Philosophy* is available in many editions.

Chapter 8 The real world

Plato's dialogue *The Republic* (many editions) contains the Analogy of the Cave. His dialogue *Parmenides* (many editions) has lots of discussion of the theory of Forms, including Plato's own objections to it. Brian Proffit's *Plato Within Your Grasp* (John Wiley & Sons, 2004) and Julia Annas's *Plato: A Very Short Introduction* ('Very Short Introductions', Oxford University Press, 2003) are suitable places to dip your toes into the ocean that is Plato's philosophy.

Chapter 9 Oranges aren't orange

Locke makes the distinction between primary and secondary qualities in his *Essay Concerning Human Understanding* (many editions). E. J. Lowe's *Locke on Human Understanding* ('Routledge Philosophy Guidebooks', Routledge, 1995) provides a very clear summary and exposition of the main themes and ideas of this monumental work.

Chapter 10 Cosmic comeuppance

Hinduism is a vast and complex subject. *Hinduism: A Beginner's Guide* ('Beginner's Guides', Oneworld Publications, 2007) by Klaus K. Klostermaier provides a clear overview; and it does a fine job of explaining the concepts of *karma*, *samsara* and *moksha*.

Chapter 11 It's all in the numbers

Pythagoras and His Theorem: The Big Idea (Arrow, 2009) by Paul Strathern is an entertaining romp through the life and ideas of Pythagoras. Although it is very brief it includes plenty of discussion about his 'everything is number' claim. Chapter 6 of *Presocratic Philosophy: A Very Short Introduction* (Oxford University Press, 2004) by Catherine Osborne provides a brief but informative introduction to the life and teachings of Pythagoras.

Chapter 12 Dan Brown vs Shakespeare

Utilitarianism and Other Essays (Penguin Classics, 2000) introduces you to utilitarianism through some of the most important writings of Jeremy Bentham and John Stuart Mill. Roger Crisp's *Routledge Philosophy Guidebook to Mill on Utilitarianism* (Routledge, 1997) is a comprehensive and interesting study of Mill's influential essay advocating utilitarianism. Chapter 2 of Crisp's book deals, in depth, with the themes discussed here.

Chapter 13 Burn, baby, burn

Augustine's *Confessions* (many editions) is one of the all-time great autobiographies. It was written during Augustine's first three years as a bishop, and is a masterpiece of literature, psychology, theology and philosophy. Augustine comes across as a tortured soul, but that makes his 'confessions' all the more compelling. *Augustine* ('Blackwell Great Minds', Wiley-Blackwell, 2004) by Gareth Matthews is a good introduction to Augustine's most important philosophical ideas. It's pitched more at the level of undergraduate or postgraduate students than the general reader, but worth persevering with.

Chapter 14 Again, and again, and again . . .

Nietzsche is a very difficult philosopher to get a handle on. *Nietzsche: A Beginner's Guide* (Oneworld Publications, reprint edn, 2010) by Robert Wicks will help you make a start. *What Nietzsche Really Said* (Schocken Books, 2001) by Robert C. Solomon and Kathleen M. Higgins also provides a comprehensive and readable overview of Nietzsche's philosophy. The idea of eternal recurrence features prominently in Nietzsche's masterpiece, *Thus Spoke Zarathustra* (many editions). In this chapter, I mention Robert C. Solomon, author of *Living With Nietzsche* (Oxford University Press, 2003).

Chapter 15 All in the mind

Berkeley writes engaging prose, so a great place to start exploring his ideas is in his own works. Check out *Principles of Human Knowledge* and *Three Dialogues between Hylas and Philonous* (available together in Penguin Classics). *Modern Philosophy: the Seventeenth and Eighteenth Centuries* ('Fundamentals of Philosophy', Routledge, 2003) by Richard

Francks does a great job of explaining Berkeley's ideas to the general reader.

Chapter 16 Now I remember

This chapter deals with ideas from Plato's *Meno* and the *Phaedo*. The two books I recommended for chapter 1 (*Protagoras and Meno* and *The Last Days of Socrates*) have both dialogues covered.

Chapter 17 Gambling on God

For general introductions to the philosophy of religion see my recommendations for chapter 7. Both of the books I recommend there include discussions of Pascal's Wager. *On Pascal* ('Wadsworth Philosophers Series', Wadsworth Publishing, 2002) by Douglas Groothuis is a good read if you want a brief and accessible summary of Pascal's life and philosophy. But bear in mind that Groothuis is a Christian philosopher and apologist, and very sympathetic to Pascal's ideas.

Chapter 18 The ghost in the machine

Descartes has been dubbed 'the father of modern philosophy'. His brief, beautiful *Meditations on First Philosophy* (many editions) is one of philosophy's all-time great works. It's an absolute must-read, and a good place to begin exploring the mind-body problem. Chapter 6 of Nigel Warburton's *Philosophy: the Basics*

(Routledge, 4th edn, 2004) is a pacy, readable introduction to the philosophy of mind. It deals with the mind-body problem and discusses a number of attempted solutions.

Chapter 19 How did that happen?

For a very thorough and clear account of Malebranche's occasionalism read chapter 5 of *The Cambridge Companion to Malebranche* ('Cambridge Companions to Philosophy', Cambridge University Press, 2000). The chapter is written by Steven Nadler, the book's editor.

Chapter 20 Leibniz's fantastic fairytale

To learn the basics about Leibniz and his ideas, see my recommended reading for chapter 2. For a thorough discussion of the *Monadology* check out the *Routledge Philosophy Guidebook to Leibniz and the Monadology* ('Routledge Philosophy Guidebooks', Routledge, 2000) by Anthony Savile. This includes the complete text of the *Monadology* itself.

Chapter 21 Ouch! I feel good

Epicureanism ('Ancient Philosophies', University of California Press, 2009) by Tim O'Keefe is a good clear introduction to the philosophy of Epicurus. There's also *The Cambridge Companion to Epicureanism* ('Cambridge Companions to

Philosophy', Cambridge University Press, 2009) if you want to delve deeper.

Chapter 22 You can't predict the future

Bertrand Russell's classic introductory guide to philosophy, *The Problems of Philosophy* (many editions), has a very good chapter on the problem of induction. The whole book is, in fact, very good. So it's worth reading all of it. Russell writes clearly and concisely, and encourages the reader to think things through every step of the way.

Chapter 23 An end to suffering

The Buddha: A Beginner's Guide (Oneworld Publications, 2009) by John Strong is a readable and stimulating introduction to the life and teachings of the Buddha. *Buddhism: A Very Short Introduction* ('Very Short Introductions', Oxford University Press, new edn, 2000) by Damien Keown is excellent too, as is *The Buddha: A Very Short Introduction* ('Very Short Introductions', Oxford University Press, new edn, 2001) by Michael Carrithers.

Chapter 24 The weaker sex?

For general background about Schopenhauer and his ideas see my suggestions for chapter 3.

All Schopenhauer quotations in this chapter are taken from the essay *On Women* in *Parerga and Paralipomena: Short Philosophical Essays from Arthur Schopenhauer, Volume 2* (Clarendon Press, new edn, 2000) translated by E. F. J. Payne. *The Philosophy of Schopenhauer* (Clarendon Press, 2nd revised edn, 1997) by Bryan Magee is very good if you want to delve more deeply into Schopenhauer. *The Cambridge Companion to Schopenhauer* ('Cambridge Companions to Philosophy', Cambridge University Press, 1999) edited by Christopher Janaway is very good, but quite an advanced text.

Chapter 25 Selfishness is a virtue

Allan Gotthelf's *On Ayn Rand* ('Wadsworth Philosophers Series', Wadsworth Publishing Co. Inc., 2000) is a brief, accessible – and unashamedly pro-Randian – summary of Ayn Rand's philosophy. For a not-so-brief statement of her ethical views try her novel, *Atlas Shrugged* (Penguin Classics, updated edn, 2007). If, after reading those, you find yourself becoming a convinced ethical egoist, read Peter Singer's *How Are We to Live?: Ethics in an Age of Self-Interest* (Oxford Paperbacks, new edn, 1997) before you quite make up your mind.

Chapter 26 One hand clapping

Eastern Philosophy: The Greatest Thinkers and Sages from Ancient to Modern Times (Arcturus Publishing, reissue edn, 2006), by

Kevin Burns, is a really good introduction to Eastern thought that focuses on philosophy rather than religion. It has a good section on Japanese philosophy.

Chapter 27 Thou shalt kill

Plato's dialogue the *Euthyphro* (many editions) introduces the Euthyphro problem when Socrates asks, 'Is the pious loved by the gods because it is pious, or is it pious because it is loved by the gods?' There's a nice, accessible discussion of Divine Command Theory in Chapter 2 of *Ethics: The Fundamentals* ('Fundamentals of Philosophy', Wiley-Blackwell, 2006) by Julia Driver. If you're interested in learning about Ockham and his ideas in general, read *Ockham Explained* ('Ideas Explained', Open Court Publishing Co., 2009) by Rondo Keele.

Chapter 28 The brain in the jar

Nigel Warburton surveys some of the philosophical problems involved in justifying our beliefs about the external world in chapter 4 of *Philosophy: The Basics* (Routledge, 4th edn, 2004). The chapter includes discussions of the brain-in-the-jar puzzle and solipsism.

Chapter 2 of Gary Cox's *How to Be a Philosopher: Or How to Be Almost Certain that Almost Nothing is Certain* (Continuum, 2010) discusses the 'evil demon' argument, and shows just how close it brought Descartes to solipsism.

Chapter 29 Harry Potter exists

Russell: A Very Short Introduction ('Very Short Introductions', Oxford University Press, 2002) by A. C. Grayling provides a good overview of Russell's life and work. It discusses Russell's contributions to philosophy and logic, and also his contributions to social, political and popular thought. Chapter 2 of Grayling's book includes an account of Russell's Theory of Descriptions which proved so devastating to Meinong's ideas about existing and subsisting.

Chapter 30 No one's to blame

Thomas Nagel's academic paper *Moral Luck* is available in an anthology entitled *Moral Luck* ('Suny Series in Ethical Theory', State University of New York Press, 1993), edited by Daniel Statman.

For a very comprehensive and thorough treatment of moral luck read *Morality, Moral Luck and Responsibility: Fortune's Web* (Palgrave Macmillan, 2005) by Nafsika Athanassoulis.

Chapter 31 Duty calls!

Kant is a great philosopher but a terrible writer. His sentences are long and cumbersome, and he uses a lot of very technical and abstruse vocabulary. Unless you have plenty of time and motivation, you are unlikely to gain much understanding of his ideas by delving straight into his books.

The best place to start, then, is with a general introduction. I recommend Roger Scruton's *Kant: A Very Short Introduction* ('Very Short Introductions', Oxford University Press, new edn, 2001). Scruton does a truly outstanding job of making Kant's very deep ideas comprehensible and interesting.

Chapter 32 Mind your behaviour

For a general introduction to the philosophy of mind, E. J. Lowe's *An Introduction to the Philosophy of Mind* ('Cambridge Introductions to Philosophy', Cambridge University Press, 2000) is very good. Chapter 3 of Edward Feser's *Philosophy of Mind: A Beginner's Guide* ('Beginner's Guides', Oneworld Publications, revised edn, 2007) includes a very clear description and discussion of behaviourism.

Chapter 33 Body-swapping

There's a good discussion of Locke's account of personal identity in chapter 6 of E. J. Lowe's *Locke on Human Understanding* ('Routledge Philosophy Guidebooks', Routledge, 1995).

Chapter 34 Cannibal conundrums

Hooked on Philosophy: Thomas Aquinas Made Easy (Alba House, 1995) by Robert A. O'Donnell is an excellent first introduction to Aquinas's thought. *Aquinas: A Beginner's Guide* ('Beginner's Guides', Oneworld, 2009) by Edward Feser is great if you're looking to delve a little deeper.

Chapter 35 Philosophy? Nonsense!

How to Read Hume (Granta Books, 2008) by Simon Blackburn is a short but good summary of Hume's thought.

The ideas discussed in this chapter come from David Hume's *An Enquiry Concerning Human Understanding* (many editions).

Hume's *Enquiry* is discussed very briefly and very well in Nigel Warburton's *Philosophy: the Classics* (Routledge, 3rd edn, 2006). This excellent book also introduces and assesses works by Plato, Aristotle, Descartes, Hobbes, Locke, Kant, Schopenhauer, Mill, Kierkegaard, Nietzsche, Russell and others.

Chapter 36 World 3

Popper discusses world 3 in chapter 38 of his *Unended Quest: An Intellectual Biography* ('Routledge Classics', Routledge, 2nd edn, 2002). There's a chapter dealing with world 3 in Bryan Magee's excellent *Popper* ('Fontana Modern Masters', Fontana Press, reissue edn, 2010).

Chapter 37 Nothing to discuss

There's a nice crisp summary of Ayer's philosophy in chapter 8 of *The British Empiricists* (Routledge, 2nd edn, 2007) by Stephen Priest. Ayer defines, explains and argues for the verification principle in the logical positivists' manifesto, *Language, Truth, and Logic* (many editions), and shows how it may be applied to traditional philosophical problems. Chapter 6 of Ayer's book contains his critique of ethics.

Chapter 38 R.I.P. God

The 'God is dead' theme appears in Nietzsche's *The Gay Science* (many editions) and in *Thus Spoke Zarathustra* (many editions).

For general introductions to Nietzsche see my recommendations for chapter 14. Both of the books I recommend there discuss the 'God is dead' claim.

Chapter 39 The ultimate vice

For books about St Thomas Aquinas and his philosophy see my recommendations for chapter 34.

Aquinas discusses the rankings of the sins of lust in *Summa Theologica* (II–II, q. 154, a. 12). The *Summa* is an enormous work, usually running to about five volumes, but it is readily available in e-book format, and there are a number of concise editions available.

Chapter 40 Rules . . . rules . . . rules . . .

For an up-to-date, well-written introduction to Taoism, check out *Daoism: A Beginner's Guide* ('Beginner's Guides', Oneworld, 2008) by James Miller.

Chapter 41 Absurd, but true

Kierkegaard ('Oneworld Philosophers', Oneworld, 2003) by Michael Watts offers a clear and concise introduction to Kierkegaard's life, writings and ideas. Chapter 3 of Watts' book deals with Kierkegaard's views on religious faith and the 'absolute paradox'. Chapter 5 of *How to Read Kierkegaard* ('How to Read', Granta Books, 2007) by John D. Caputo summarises and discusses Kierkegaard's *Philosophical Fragments* and *Concluding Unscientific Postscript*.

Chapter 42 Scientifically unproven

For an introduction to Karl Popper and his ideas try Bryan Magee's brief but brilliant *Popper* ('Fontana Modern Masters', Fontana Press, reissue edn, 2010). For an introduction to the philosophy of science try A. F. Chalmers' *What Is This Thing Called Science?* (Open University Press, 3rd edn, 1999). It's a fascinating read for anyone who's at all interested in the history of science.

Chapter 43 The unexamined life

Plato's dialogue, the *Apology*, is available in *The Last Days of Socrates* (Penguin Classics, 2010), which was one of my recommended books for chapter 1.

There's a very good chapter about Socrates' 'unexamined life' claim in *A Companion to Socrates* ('Blackwell Companions to Philosophy', Wiley-Blackwell, 2009), edited by Sara Ahbel-Rappe and Rachana Kamtekar. The chapter I'm referring to is chapter 14, entitled 'The Examined Life', written by Richard Kraut.

INDEX